The Death Within

> How do mainstream beliefs and socially accepted norms cause mental distress in teenagers?
>
> This book explains!

By

Hamayun Khan

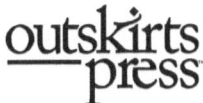

The Death Within
All Rights Reserved.
Copyright © 2023 Hamayun Khan
v5.0 r1.2

The opinions expressed in this manuscript are solely the opinions of the author and do not represent the opinions or thoughts of the publisher. The author has represented and warranted full ownership and/or legal right to publish all the materials in this book.

This book may not be reproduced, transmitted, or stored in whole or in part by any means, including graphic, electronic, or mechanical without the express written consent of the publisher except in the case of brief quotations embodied in critical articles and reviews.

Outskirts Press, Inc.
http://www.outskirtspress.com

ISBN: 978-1-9772-4813-8

Cover Photo © 2023 Hamayun Khan. All rights reserved - used with permission.

Outskirts Press and the "OP" logo are trademarks belonging to Outskirts Press, Inc.

PRINTED IN THE UNITED STATES OF AMERICA

Starting in the name of the Almighty (exalted be his name) the creator of the creatures, the owner of hearts, the sole might, the one, the eternal king, & the divine being to whom all praises belong.

Acknowledgments

I BEGAN WORKING on this book in 2019, just before the COVID-19 pandemic. Since childhood, I have been prone to suppressing my sentiments while dealing with my inner agony, however. When I realized I could not find someone who could genuinely listen to and understand the inner me, I decided that writing those sentiments down would be an effective way to help cope with the inner anguish.

This book is mainly based on my observations and experiences. My words of real-life stories with fictional characters inspired the stories that I have penned to help explain my ideas. The main objective for authoring this book is first to expose today's youth's suppressed sentiments and voices and the significant elements that stifle their inner peace. As someone who has experienced emotional despair and mental suffering, most youth today share the same experience and lack of inner peace.

Therefore, I dedicate this book, especially to myself – my inner soul, and to all the teenagers whose minds and souls are overflowing with tolerance, compassion, and empathy and that would prefer to tolerate mental suffering to protect socially accepted beliefs and codes rather than debating about those beliefs that might offend the followers.

I owe my dear friend Zabihullah Shahrani for his help with designing the book's cover pages. I also want to express my profound thanks to a handful of my close friends who share my perspectives and life experiences. I am grateful to a handful of my like-minded friends for constantly sharing their life experiences with me and encouraging me to author this book. I wish them peace.

Life is not a race for success but a quest for satisfaction. Gaining satisfaction is real success and happiness. If we face troubles while achieving satisfaction, we mentally suffer, leading us to feel inner pain – which I call the death within. Therefore, I hope this book will enable its readers, particularly the younger ones, to grasp the importance of inner peace and prioritize it to avoid internal sorrow. The book, therefore, identifies the primary causes of inner suffering, which makes a person, a teenager in particular, more prone to burying their sentiments within - even when that person desperately wants to express them.

– *Hamayun Khan*

Table of Contents

Author's Note 1
Why This Book? 3
SECTION A – INNER PEACE MATTERS 7
   Inner Peace 9
   The Lack of Inner Peace 33
SECTION – B. HOMES PLAY A ROLE 57
   Home is a Prison 59
   Emotional Connection 64
   Self-Esteem 83
   Parental Role 92
   Females' Vulnerability 99
SECTION – C. HAZARDOUS SOCIETY 105
   Societal Codes 107
   Psychological Enslavement 124
   Emotional Distress 131
   The Exploitation of Social Status 140
   Bibliography 151

Author's Note

SEVERAL BACKWARD NATIONS have emphasized mainstream societal beliefs more than reason and intellect. One of the main reasons such civilizations are constantly backward in terms of technology and industrialization is that they are not ready to accept thinking critically, debating the validity of their ideas, and readily accepting change, even if that change is novel and does not conflict with their values or harm them. Because they think that their societies' backwardness is a sign of true testament to their sincere faith in upholding their ancestors' principles of life, the inhabitants of these civilizations frequently feel complacent about their lives in a static form. These people also desire to resemble their ancestors' way of life and maintain it by adhering to their old codes, which is at odds with our rapidly changing world today and its ineluctable emerging dynamics. I am not arguing that those old codes are wrong, but those codes were best applicable to the time of our forebears and not the fast-paced, 4.0 industrialized world.

People from backward societies also adhere to a belief system heavily influenced by being required to revere their elders and social and religious leaders to maintain their eternal faith. However, this phenomenon frequently impacts today's teenagers in terms of their inner peace, behavior, and way of life. From a distinct perspective, people in those societies emphasize maintaining the fundamental beliefs of their ancestors over making beneficial changes, even if those beliefs conflict with the laws of the dynamic world or require them to remain in the past. People, for instance, continue to lead the same lifestyle as their forebears. They regard their life as only a little adventure because they think the advanced lifestyle of earthly existence has no significance. This is why they live the centuries-old routine.

Individuals from backward societies never dare to examine anything connected to their ingrained views, so they remain psychologically static in their daily life. As a result, those who adhere to the essential beliefs of their ancestors continue to be psychologically shackled and lead a constrained lifestyle with little capacity for critical or unconventional thinking in today's advanced world. This narrative is, regrettably, centuries old. Therefore, it is evident that wherever there has been a dearth of understanding and intelligence throughout the history of humanity, I am confident that clever misinterpretations of religious doctrines and widespread belief systems have likely always been successful strategies to subjugate populations, rule over them, and amass wealth. Because of this, ordinary people suffer, particularly those who can think critically and have unconventional viewpoints yet are restricted from speaking.

Why This Book?

MANY BOOKS ARE available on the discussion of mental wellness and inner peace. Unquestionably, reading those books will expose one to a wealth of significant insights regarding mental health.

Subjective in nature, in the case of this book, The Death Within, one significant factor distinguishing it from other books is the way it exposes the unacknowledged mental problems arising from real-life events that harm many teenagers, particularly in underdeveloped civilizations, i.e., Afghanistan. Afghanistan is used as an example to illustrate the central philosophy of the book. Thus, the argument in the book is reinforced by the fact that around ninety-nine percent of Afghans practice Islam alongside a strong belief in cultural norms. Because of this, most Afghans' everyday choices are influenced by and based on social standards and religious principles.

Additionally, Afghanistan has endured long-running wars and political unrest that have destroyed its institutions and led to its eventual emergence as a third-world country. Because of such backwardness, a significant percentage of the current generation—including well-educated youngsters with access to technology and information—experience mental pain at an early age. This is primarily due to the disconnect between the modern perspective of teenagers and the attitudes of their elders, whose philosophies have been influenced by religion and social circles.

This does not imply a fault with culture or religious beliefs; rather, it indicates an issue with how religious and cultural principles, rules, and values are taught, perceived, and applied. Contrary to fundamental spiritual matters, such laws and standards are frequently violated and enforced with coercion. However, in the Holy Quran, Allah SWT commands the believers, "There shall be no coercion in issues of faith" (2:256). This implies that Islam (the majorly followed religion in Afghanistan) does not support any form of force on a person's free choice to adhere to Islam or any other faith or religion.

Besides, even though introverted teenagers frequently find it challenging to communicate their emotions, when they are made to do something which they may not necessarily want to do, they become mentally depressed. Anxiety brought on by such emotional anguish even prompts suicide in some cases. The leading causes of mental distress in teenagers, according to this book, are self-adopted behavior and fear of being perceived as a sinner or a nonbeliever or disobedient as per religion and culture, social codes being subtly imposed, the discrepancy between a teenager's mindset and that of their families, forced respect, and the exploitation of religious & societal norms and principles. In this sense, personal behavior refers to the decision to put up with mental suffering rather than break accepted social norms and harm others. When a family's lifestyle is out of step with a teenager's view and behavior, who grows up in a different era, a generation gap gradually forms between their mindsets and behaviors. On the other hand, most social elements are based on false and superstitious codes enforced to favor the upper class of society at the expense of many others, particularly teenagers.

This book, therefore, emphasizes the value of inner peace, mental fulfillment, and happiness, which teens today, particularly those from middle-class households in underdeveloped cultures, need the most. I have used real-life-based subjective experiences and factual tales to support the argument to better highlight the topic matter. The book also provides many examples of various aspects that show how teenagers get mentally troubled and sad. Overall, teens frequently commit suicide due to their harmful mental torment. And as a result, a lot of teenagers' lives end, which is worrying. The cause is frequently the naive faith of people in myths or superstitions subtly presented as religious doctrines, duties, or socially acceptable codes imposed on youth.

Given these realities, it is crucial to comprehend the issues listed above that prevent youth from experiencing inner peace. Additionally, it is essential to identify the underlying reasons for the case of today's teens—such as anxiety—which is equally important to address. The awkward thing about this problem is that it is not always possible to convey it clearly to anyone, even to close friends and family members like best friends or parents. Most of the time, such mental illnesses are kept secret in the heart and mind, which causes teenagers to die on the inside. Inclined by such emotional and mental suffering, this book serves as the voice of many suffering teenagers, particularly the sensitive and introverted ones.

SECTION – A.
INNER PEACE MATTERS

In this book section, I have covered the critical need for inner peace among teenagers and a few common obstacles to the desire to gain mental peace. For this purpose, I have recounted actual incidents, observations, and experiences pertinent to the subject to further enhance the book's content. This part is divided into two sub-sections; the first sub-section discusses the importance of inner peace and how to obtain it. The second sub-section addresses the impediments to achieving inner peace.

Inner Peace

"To be stupid, selfish, and have good health are three requirements for happiness, though if stupidity is lacking, all is lost."
– Gustave Flaubert –

WHILE THE COMMON saying "Health is Wealth" lends great credence to the above proverb, which emphasizes the importance of foolishness, greed, and good health for happiness. But the quote's folly, selfishness, and good health denote emotional freedom, obsession with oneself, and physical vigor. However, the quote's creator, Gustave Flaubert, underlines the significance of stupidity. In his quotation, he views the lack of absurdity as the absence of other factors (e.g., good health and selfishness). On the other hand, based on how I interpret the quote, each element that orchestrates happiness's significance is equally relevant.

If good health is essential for inner peace, then stupidity should equally be at the top of the list of one's priorities. This includes the absurdity that most people dislike and find unfair and the freedom to follow their dreams, make their own decisions, and live their life however they desire and whatever makes them happy. Similarly, selfishness does not necessarily indicate naughtiness or rudeness; instead, it may indicate a drive to simply accept to "be you"—to love, accept, and impress oneself with one's actions. While doing so, it may not always be crucial to know what other people think of you or whether they are impressed by your activities. Worrying about what others may say or think is less significant when you know you are correct and when your inner self does not hold you accountable. Because achieving inner peace requires that we be content with who we are.

However, situations can get tricky at times. Still, using your inherent skills to transform adversity into an opportunity is essential. For example, doors may close at a certain point, and life may become difficult sometimes, but if a door you desire is closed, simply try to open it. However, double-check that you are opening the right door while doing so. If a door is locked, locate the keys, and double-check that you have the proper keys. Finding the right door, however, is more crucial than finding the perfect keys since if you have the correct keys but are unsure which door to enter, you are on the incorrect route. As a result, it is critical to first ensure you know which door to open; only then will it be simpler to find the correct keys and unlock the door.

For example, suppose there are two people, A and B. Both of them graduate from the same field and go for an interview. While A and B graduate from the same area, they possess different skills. For instance, person A maintains the interpersonal skills required to be an ideal candidate for the proposed job. He is still determining how and where to use them. The same person, for example, constantly needs to think about whether the job he interviews for will be the right place for his career growth, which takes up much of his time.

On the other hand, person B only possesses as many interpersonal skills as person A. However, person B holds the trait of persistence. Unlike person A, one of person B's weaknesses is that he is a slow learner. However, he constantly employs his lone characteristic of perseverance, which allows him to act and keep things going rather than waste time pondering.

Person A is now perplexed by unneeded thoughts before and after the interview since he still determines whether the company is a good fit for him. As a result, he loses his attention and overthinks if he could only do better in the interview. Even if he does well and is offered the role, he will still be unable to focus on his job since he will be wasting his time constantly pondering about his career. Nonetheless, person B will tend to focus on his job and work hard during and after the interview. Because person B understands that the job, he is interviewing for is the best place for him to advance his career. Even if it is not the right place for him, he may make it so by learning and gaining experience. Even if person B fails the interview and is not hired, he will continue to seek other jobs. In case of a failure, person A, on the other hand, will overthink acquiring the perfect job at the right place rather than focusing on applying his skills. As a result, he will be unable to use his gained abilities practically.

A and B have the same degree, but I choose B, the slow learner with perseverance. Person A's quick learning skills are keys, in this case, indicating that he possesses the correct keys. Person B needs to gain the necessary keys: sharp learning abilities. Still, he understands where to go and how to turn his lack of skills into efficiency. Another vital attribute has been the ability to use precise timing, which is essential in life; for example, understanding how to complete everything perfectly at the appropriate time and location. Overall, this can make a person feel more content. The most essential thing a person will ever need is inner peace, which is the ultimate objective, unparalleled achievement, and above everything else.

Also, for some people, spirituality is a source of inner peace. For instance, to find inner peace, they passionately believe in and faithfully adhere to religious teachings – irrespective of having a thorough knowledge of those principles. Such people believe that putting aside all other materialistic pursuits would lead to inner pleasure because it is possible to connect with divinity through spirituality which helps gain inner peace.

Because when they fulfill a religious commitment, even in destitution, they feel inner content and joyful. Even their usual failures will not deter such individuals from finding inner peace since they have lost dependence on materialism. They view failure and success as two distinct sides of the same coin, according to what I have witnessed of such folks. So, they quickly deal with both success and failure in their daily lives, and neither impacts their ability to be at peace with themselves.

The fundamental reason is their commitment to spirituality and divinity, which makes them less interested in materialism. Even based on my perspective, success and failure should be seen as learning opportunities since experience always engenders learning. So, both our successes and failures teach us something. Overall, success and failure need to be seen as minor aspects of our lives rather than the basis for our ability to maintain inner peace.

Another group of individuals also practices an odd method of gaining mental peace. To achieve mental peace, this group of people is even willing to give up their current level of happiness. These individuals, for instance, can intend to establish a benchmark for themselves to be happy within. For instance, they set a benchmark of happiness for themselves by thinking that after that objective was accomplished, they would then go on a trip or picnic with friends or family. Or they give up on good nutrition, fashionable attire, or enough rest until they reach their goal. With such thoughts in mind, such people definitely will feel pleased once their set out objectives are attained. Until then their objectives will keep them constantly agitated. Nevertheless, humans should put their inner peace first. Since no goal in life can reach the level of importance of inner peace as achieving objectives is part of the process and not the end goal. While inner peace is the end goal.

Therefore, our inner peace and mental health are so significant that our careers, employment, academic degrees, friends, goals, money, houses, and relatives cannot compare. Because nothing else will feel well, and nothing matters if one's spirit is troubled and not at peace. By achieving our goals, we may or may not favor ourselves but most often our sole intention remains being ahead in the societal race and to impress society – even if it cost us our peace. The reason is that if someone believes that sacrificing their inner peace to impress or please others is a sign of humanity, they are utterly mistaken.

Suppose such an individual, on the one hand, earns the admiration of others. In that case, he or she is also, inadvertently, severely oppressing himself or herself - let alone caring for humanity. Therefore, we must first be faithful to our inner peace, and then we can deal with the outside world more effectively.

Since inner peace is crucial, it is equally important to understand its definition. While every person in the world has a distinct description of inner peace concerning real-life problems. Every definition of these difficulties relating to one's mental and physical health, which comes from personal experience or observation, is correct. Suppose a person defines something precisely yet differently based on a personal encounter with an event. In that case, it is valid from their perspective — and perhaps from the perspectives of many others as well.

For me, inner peace simply refers to the satisfaction one feels within. It may be attained by two essential factors: the first is solicited, and the second is unsolicited. Inner peace holds a special place in many people's lives. Although I consider inner peace incredibly positive, I still think it should be attained constructively. By constructively I mean in a way that does not physically or psychologically harm other people. Because it will directly impact one's own inner peace, when he gains mental satisfaction with the cost of harming other people.

On the other hand, others view the process of gaining inner peace from a unique perspective. Such people, for example, do not care one bit about whether the method or source they use to get inner peace is terrible, hurtful, exemplary, or advantageous to others. Such people frequently achieve inner peace and satisfaction through destructive practices to other people's mental health. Still, they have yet to give this fact any consideration. Comedians are the most typical example.

Even though comedians make jokes that frequently hurt other people's feelings, they still joke about individuals. The reason is that a comedian takes pleasure in telling jokes when the audience laughs because he believes that doing so makes the people around him happy. However, he needs to learn about the other side of the coin. Which is that his jokes could also hurt a person's feelings who take the jokes for serious.

Generally speaking, I have seen individuals using the most popular tactics to find interior peace, as shown in Figure 1. psychologists, anthropologists, and specialists in human behavior may have found several additional variables, nonetheless. Their scientific theories and hypotheses might point to different causes of people's inner peace-seeking. However, I have been exposed to a situation where individuals behave in real life.

For example, some people might have a distinct temperament, mindset, and way of life. Others may have a different perspective on life. Some might have a view that is inspired by a belief in upstanding morals and values.

Based on such subjective observation, I have concluded that "solicited" and "unsolicited" are the two main variables that serve as sources of inner peace. The former offers deliberate approaches, whereas the latter offers unintentional, inadvertent methods. The former occurs due to a person's inherent behavior and actions. In contrast, the latter occurs primarily as a result of external factors or, to put it another way, as a result of the behavior and actions of others.

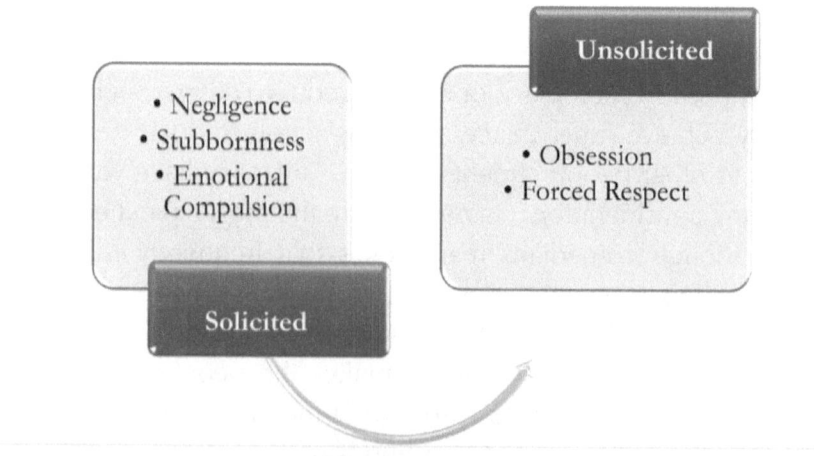

Figure 1. Approaches that are used to achieve inner peace.

Solicited:

Life frequently brings us to a stage where we feel obligated to work diligently toward achieving mental peace. For this to happen, we would skip doing certain tasks and instead do some other tasks. However, we would attempt either one. It frequently happens that we do not know we are trying to find inner peace while working to get mental peace. This phenomenon will persist until such a time as we comprehend the value of inner peace and how to achieve it. In the end, we make an intentional effort to stay away from things that we believe will disturb our mental health.

There are various techniques that humans use to achieve peace through solicited means. These techniques include consciously avoiding particular individuals or changing one's behavior to manage critical issues that might prohibit them from feeling inner peace. This is done intentionally, allowing a person to take a preplanned action. Techniques that can help achieve peace through solicited means include mindfulness meditation or deep breathing exercises.

Readers can better understand the concepts being discussed by breaking down content into smaller paragraphs and using subheadings to organize the text. Providing concrete examples can also help readers apply the concepts to their lives. Lastly, including practical tips or strategies for managing stress and anxiety can make the text more actionable and helpful for readers looking to improve their mental health.

Negligence:

Intentionally ignoring anything important, critical, or psychologically related to one's thinking is one of the most challenging acts for a person to accomplish. For instance, most of the time, when we encounter a difficult or unimportant situation that may endanger our mental tranquility. We make efforts to avoid that. Suppose we do not face a situation or decide independently. In that case, we refer to our friends to help us encounter or eliminate the issues harming our mental peace.

Therefore, our friends constantly advise us to clear a particular problem, or, on occasion, they make suggestions for solutions that are more likely to simply sidestep the issue. At the same time, we are stuck in a decision-making conundrum. However, one cannot mentally force another person to do or not do something, especially if they are not genuinely self-motivated to do so. This might result from one's inherent attitude, which is always in the other direction and works against one's aims.

Most of the time, we unconsciously avoid mentally challenging circumstances that we might not want to face or are not mentally prepared to manage. In light of this, a common saying goes, "Enjoy what you do and do what you enjoy." This quote is included because it is accurate to say that our mental health can significantly affect our bodily and psychological well-being. This is because most people work in professions, they do not particularly like but are compelled to do so because they have to earn money.

It's important to acknowledge that work can significantly impact mental health. While some individuals may find fulfillment in their job, others may struggle with low-paying or unsatisfying work. Additionally, some people may feel pressure to work in a specific field for financial reasons, even if it's not a good fit for their abilities or interests. This can lead to mental health issues such as depression, as the stress of the job takes a toll on their well-being. It's crucial to prioritize mental health and seek support when needed, whether finding a new job or seeking professional help.

It's also essential to be adaptable and open-minded while interacting with teenagers. Sometimes, we must trust our gut instincts and adjust our perspectives to establish a connection with them and build a friendship. Once we've gained their trust, getting them to see things from our point of view and understand what we're asking of them becomes more straightforward. This same principle applies in a corporate setting as well.

It's essential to be aware of the behavior of those around us and find a way to fit in or feel comfortable in our workplace environment.

We can't always expect others to cater to our needs and desires, so it's essential to be flexible and willing to adapt.

In the case of a child, even though a child might not be interested in certain things, his elders and parents will make him have them and appreciate them. In other situations, parents may even punch or become enraged with their children, but later they will give in to their children's requests.

This means parents show anger and irritation that get instilled in their children's psyche before giving them what they want just to pacify them. In this situation, the parents feel they are helping their children. However, their actions will utterly shatter their children's fragile mental peace. Eventually, their children will also come to despise their parents. Impacting both their behavior and personality. For children, being treated poorly by parents while parents try their best to please their children is just as detrimental as maintaining animosity with those children.

As a result, sometimes, we must follow our instincts and change our perspectives to fit in with the kids. This way, we can gain their trust and start a friendship. After that, we can easily have them accept what we want from them and make them understand certain things. This applies to corporate work as well. We need to fit in with the behavior of others in the workplace atmosphere or find a setting in which we feel at ease. Because we cannot always have our behavior accepted and demands fulfilled by others.

It is, therefore, crucial to avoid feeling pressured to complete a particular activity or solve a specific problem to maintain our mental well-being. Studies have shown that pursuing various methods to find inner peace is ineffective and can lead to mental depression inclined by obsession with finding inner peace. Instead of forcing ourselves to calm down, we should focus on finding ways to combat the indirect pressure that causes our minds to suffer.

This is crucial, especially when trying to prevent stress from being put on our minds to worry about completing a particular activity or averting a specific problem. The fact that so many people experience mental depression shows that their belief that they can find inner peace by pursuing various methods is not promising. Rather than enhancing our mental calm, this exercise exerts indirect pressure on the mind that causes it to suffer.

Stubbornness:

One of the most widely criticized human characteristics is stubbornness. However, according to my experience, stubbornness can actually have a positive impact on one's psychological health. For instance, when the intention to achieve a desired goal or accomplish a particular task is fueled by self-centered or egotistical determination, it can frequently produce favorable outcomes.

To illustrate this point, let me narrate here about a friend of mine who was obstinate yet always on the right track. Despite struggling with his studies, he refused to give up and was determined to succeed. He overcame his challenges by seeking help, studying harder, and never losing sight of his goals. His stubbornness and perseverance towards achieving his goals ultimately led to his success. Thus, it is important to note that while stubbornness can be beneficial in certain situations, it is also essential to be empathetic and understanding towards others who may be struggling. Being patient and supportive to others can go a long way in helping someone achieve their goals.

Because my friend constantly believed he could not perform well on school examinations, he always prepared himself for sports. I was the only one who consistently pushed him to study despite everything else. Even though he was frequently psychologically unprepared to do so, he occasionally decided to passionately study for the sake of our friendship, as I would encourage him a lot. Sometimes he would lament to me about the disrespectful actions of his elders and friends who made fun of him for doing poorly on school examinations – as he would get discouraged and sad by such behavior.

As a result, he would feel more distanced from school. One of his friends had a reputation for being a braggart who would constantly make fun of my friend for his academic shortcomings. I avoided that arrogant boy for this reason alone. Yet I had received no damage from that boy. But why my friend put up with him for so long without even retaliating against his derision was a mystery to me. Nevertheless, my friend once shocked me with his unusual response to the criticism he received from his friends.

I remember playing cricket at a nearby playground with my friend and one of his relatives who was quite a haughty boy. After the toss, my friend was designated to bat, while his relative, who was a bit snobbish, was chosen to bowl. As for me, I was picked to be the wicketkeeper since I was the second to bat after my friend. We used a locally developed method to decide who would bat and bowl, among other things. For instance, one of the boys would voluntarily grab the bat and anchor it to the ground while facing away from the others. This boy would then draw lines on the ground to correspond with the total number of players, including himself. Finally, the boy would write numbers beneath each line.

If there are four players altogether, that volunteer boy will randomly write numbers below each line that will look randomly like 4, 2, 3, or 1. He then uses the bat to cover the numbers, revealing only the lines. He invites the other players to arrive and choose a line. As a result, once each player selects a line, the leftover line automatically belongs to the player chosen for drawing lines and numbers. When everything is said and done, the volunteer boy removes the bat from the concealed numbers to reveal who received the first turn, the second turn, and so on. After that, the turn is determined based on the secret numbers beneath each chosen line. Let us say that player A selects the line that corresponds to one, in which case he would bat first, followed by player B who chooses the line that fits two. The person who bats last will be picked to bowl first, followed by the person who bats second to last, and so on.

The first over, which entailed six deliveries, was bowled by my friend's relative, the arrogant boy. Afterward, I had to go bowling to my friend while his relative went to stand behind the wicket. Before I bowled the first delivery, I heard that the conversation between my friend and his arrogant relative suddenly began, and it was progressively heated. I had to take a break from bowling to approach them and investigate the situation. As usual, they discussed my friend's low score in seventh grade, as I understood. Because of his subpar achievement on the school exam, the conceited guy demeaned my friend and infuriated him. So, when that arrogant boy stigmatized my friend, he responded angrily, which caused their conversation to get heated and almost culminate in a fight. Due to my friend's angry response to his arrogant relative's stigma, their discussion became heated. They might have gotten into a physical altercation if I had not intervened promptly.

After I resolved the issue, my friend remained silent for a while before standing up abruptly. He vowed to punish the arrogant boy in his studies since he was so upset by the arrogant boy's harsh remarks. My friend added he would never find peace until he outperforms that arrogant boy in studies and academic achievements. Even though my friend had always doubted his capacity to succeed in his studies. Surprisingly, everything for my friend took an unexpected turn shortly after that. Until now, he had consistently outperformed his friend in all facets of life—not just academics. Therefore, his inherent quality of "stubbornness" would receive all the credit for his achievements. This is because of his innate behavior that he would do anything once he had determined. This was the time when my friend's inborn stubbornness altered his life forever.

My friend's family eventually relocated to Kabul, Afghanistan's capital, and most developed city in the country, after several years had passed. Before this, they were living in our village as refugees in Khyber Pakhtunkhwa - a pashtun-populated province across the durand line in Pakistan. I subsequently discovered that he had accomplished a lot in Kabul, including graduating from high school and earning two certificates, one in English and one in Algebra coaching programs. Considering his poor English and Math skills, I was shocked when I learned he had Math and English credentials. I came upon him on Facebook one day after setting up an account in 2015.

During childhood, he always complained that Math and English were his two least favorite courses. Thus, I could not believe his success in these disciplines. But after sending him a message in Pashto and getting a solid answer in English, I began to feel astonished.

Further strengthening my faith in his accomplishments, I later stalked his Facebook account and saw images of him carrying his certificates. I found out later that he had taken one Math class and three English coaching courses and had performed the best among his peers in English and Math. In grade twelve, he also achieved the ninth-best rank in his class. Seeing my friend excelling in the things he formerly detested and was most afraid of made me feel both proud and shocked at the same time.

After a few days had gone by and we had had enough of talking to one another on Facebook Messenger. I had visited Kabul and was expecting my friend to meet me and show me around Kabul. However, he was so terribly busy that he did not send me a message until Thursday night, inviting me to dinner that night. My friend had chosen to spend Thursday evening with me because Friday was a day off so that we could both spend time together and remember our childhood.

I accepted his invitation for the dinner, and he then told me the location of his institute, where he had attended coaching courses in Math and English. When I got a cab and made my way to Shahr-e-Naw, the center of Kabul and the home of many foreign organizations and educational institutions, it was after 4:00 pm. Because there was little traffic, I arrived at the destination on time. Since all of the workers in Shahr-e-Naw leave for home at 4:00 pm, Kabul city usually gets too overcrowded at that time. I was fortunate to have arrived there on time. I did not know where my childhood friend was when I arrived at the institution. I inquired about my friend, and the receptionist's response astounded me. The phrase "sahib," often used to show profound respect for senior citizens, high-ranking officials, and other influential individuals in Afghanistan, was used to refer to my friend by the receptionist.

After the receptionist escorted me to a room with a sizable group of students—around a hundred—I was shocked to find my friend speaking eloquently and confidently in English in front of such a sizable group of students. At the same time, everyone else outside had maintained a pin-drop decorum. I remained outside the door for a few minutes, silently staring at him through the door glass window. It was not until later that I realized I was bawling because that proud moment reminded me of the bragging and stigmatizing words of the arrogant relative of my friend. This arrogant boy would often trash my friend for doing poorly on tests.

My friend abruptly stopped talking and hurried up to me when he saw me through the door's little window after I waved my hand to him. He stayed in front of me for a while after leaving the classroom, burst into tears, and then unexpectedly began to give me a long embrace. I was thrilled when he immediately continued by whispering in my right ear that he was a teacher of English. After telling me the fantastic news, I hugged him again and congratulated him on his accomplishment. I was pleased with him, not because he had landed a lucrative job as an English teacher. Still, instead because of his perseverance in overcoming the obstacle he had always feared and suffered shame for. We exchanged greetings and then departed for a restaurant together.

My friend and I discussed our childhood experiences on the way to a restaurant. I gave him high accolades for all of his accomplishments throughout our talk. Suddenly, I remembered how his haughty relative had shamed him for performing poorly on his school exam at that very same time. It was a wise move to bring up his conceited relative to get him to reveal the secret of his success and tenacity. My friend had every single event of his childhood which greatly astonished me.

He claimed that when his conceited relative shamed him for getting a bad grade, he began to cry nonstop and made plans to end his life since he felt like a worthless, insignificant, and underrated creature. He said that his arrogant relative's and his own family's demoralizing remarks about his capacity to receive a poor grade had left him feeling too disheartened and convinced that there was nothing he could achieve with his life. Following that, he felt the urge to push himself, challenge, and do the things he was afraid that other people would find amusing. This is because he had determined that until he did not prove his family members and his arrogant relative wrong, he would not sit calmly and peacefully.

He said, "adopting a new attitude and behavior of dedication and hard work at first was difficult and stressful." Later, though, he gradually adapted to being tenacious, diligent, and capable of meeting and surmounting obstacles. Even the news that he had received a full Indian scholarship to attend Bengaluru University, one of India's top universities, as an undergraduate student further astounded me. I was utterly speechless when I learned about each accomplishment made by my friend. Due to this, I became lost in a sea of thoughts about my friend's determination, tenacity, and stubbornness, wondering how he turned his obstinacy into success and how his incompetence was transformed into challenging work. I realized that his negatively perceived behavior had eventually helped him find mental peace.

My friend's story leads us to conclude that stubbornness cannot always be a ubiquitous trait but a solicited and occasional one inclined by a human's ego and the demand of a particular situation. Sometimes, it is important to be stubborn to prove yourself right, and the other person, who does not believe in you or mocks you for your inability, is wrong. But remember, save your valuable time proving yourself right, which the other person never cares about. Instead, try to prove yourself by giving yourself time and value and developing your personality so the other person will indirectly be proved wrong. Sometimes, that person will even start following you – which is another victory for you over him. This will be a win-win game for you. Nonetheless, pushing your stubbornness with the right decision and coherent conciseness is equally essential to avoid unwanted ramifications and find inner peace.

Emotional Compulsion:

Forced and inclined by emotions, humans with sensitive nature tend to ponder everything that occurs around them or happens to them. However, such people consider everything because they desperately seek inner peace. But sometimes, overthinking leads humans to lose their way to achieving inner peace. This is why overthinking is the biggest hurdle to mental peace. Such a category of humans uses many ways to get inner peace, such as avoiding unwanted situations. Suppose someone were to tell them something or harm them in some other way. They will begin thinking about it immediately and attempting to determine the motivation behind those words and actions.

One of the leading causes of this behavior may be how these individuals express their emotions and stress themselves out when acting or speaking, as they do not want to give up on their inner peace by argumentation. They are even ready to accept the fault of others and get blamed just to be at peace. Additionally, this behavior has several facets; one is a person's tendency to attempt to please others by contemplating everything and seeking every possible way, despite being harmful to that person's mental health. Another side describes a person's inclination to intentionally avoid indulging in conflicts to prove themselves right to get mental peace.

There is another type of people who may get inner peace due to their deep-rooted emotions attached to the specific phenomenon, rituals, other norms, etc. I alluded to practices and standards as the source of some people's attempts to avoid confrontation. Since I have seen several instances of individuals taking advantage of others by invoking religious beliefs to force them to do certain tasks. The victims would naturally prepare their thinking to carry out a particular activity without giving rise to adverse reactions.

However, the victims are implicitly fearful of those religious principles being violated. Therefore, they readily agree to perform the expected task with great care. Considering that they may suffer severe consequences hereafter if they do not accomplish the desired job, these people do not believe they will ever have mental peace.

Not only that, but several other factors, such as cultural, social, and ethical principles, drive a person's inclination to intentionally seek peace of mind. Sometimes, people associate their happiness with norms or principles – as described above. While observing or following those principles, these people tend to feel happier deep within. In some South Asian countries, especially Afghanistan, people are more attached to religious and cultural norms, irrespective of how manipulated these norms could be. People more tied to religion and culture tend to blindly follow whatever is said to them with a reference from a religious book or cultural norms. This is why those people can be easily made to do a task or accept any command using the name of religion or culture.

The problem with such people is that they are least bothered about studying things on their own and researching to find out if whatever is said to them is true. However, the reason for such blind faith is that such people are more mentally peaceful as they relate every situation either to divine destiny or the devil's temptations. For example, if they experience a good condition, they think it was destined by God or was God's plan. But if they face any hardship, they will start blaming the devil (Satan) for that hardship. Taking responsibility off their shoulders makes them feel satisfied as they think their whole life goes on due to either devil's temptation or God's planned destiny.

Nevertheless, Allah in the Holy Quran mentions that whatever consequences we (humans) face are because of our own will and intention. This is because the general nature of divine providence, decree, and destiny is presented in the Qur'an so that it never conflicts with human free will and choice. The below verse is one of several verses that have raised significant questions about human free will. Per the Holy Quran, humans are accessible regarding willingness, intentions, and decision-making. However, they are bound to the divine law of causation. Indeed, such divine law is merely for the benefit of humans. This is true in terms of mental peace as well.

For instance, when we connect ourselves to the divine power and let that divine power take care of everything, we find inner peace. Here is how, for instance, most of our problems and dissatisfaction come from our desires to achieve materialistic pleasure – which is impossible to fulfill. But we find inner peace when we replace our worldly desires with spiritual desires by attaching ourselves to the laws of divine power. This is because materialistic desires are always inclined by the fight between heart and mind. The mind suffers from unfulfilled desires, and the soul suffers rampant emotions bent by those desires. Coming to the main point, below is the verse from chapter 3 and verse number 182 of the Holy Quran about humans' free will.

– This is in recompense for what your own hands have already sent, as well as proof that Allah is completely righteous toward His servants. (3:182)

The above verse of the Holy Quran demonstrates that God does not declare that the punishment was a result of the servants' activities so that in the hereafter, people might respond, "We were not free in our actions," but instead that it was because of the actions that humans took of their own free will, with no coercion. God gave humans free will when He created them. This simply means that we (humans) are to be blamed for our deeds, not God. If God had committed the act, the penalty for our deeds would be unfair.

This indicates that someone has sinned, and the sentence placed on someone else is incorrect. Because God will not treat his servants unequally. This verse also teaches us that God never treats His servants harshly. Here, two nuances should be noted: God showed His compassion using the word "servant." How, then, can God mistreat his servant? A servant deserves sympathy because of his servitude. It is inconceivable that the All-Powerful God would feel the need to mistreat a dependent and feeble servant.

However, there are differences in Muslim interpretations of religious teachings. For instance, people dispute with one another and label one another as false or errant believers if they contradict each other's views or beliefs. This is because of the need for more in-depth information and comprehension of religious teachings. As a result, most disputes between Muslim groups in nations like Afghanistan start when one group violates another group's religious or cultural values.

Without intending to offend anyone's religion or culture, it is regrettable that certain people, who have little understanding of their religion and culture, stir up more religious conflicts and animosity for people from various backgrounds. Religions and cultures are harmed more by their adherents than by those of other faiths.

Their limited knowledge and lack of cognizance have molded their minds like a blank paper, on which anything disguised as religious principles, can be written. They are least bothered about the authencity of those words. Because they are unable to critically think as their minds have been constrained by superstitious beliefs and apprehended with the unseen torment.

Thus, we should not let our emotions prevent us from being mentally peaceful. Additionally, we should not be emotionally coerced to either accept or reject certain traits that can harm our happiness and mental peace. But instead of being dependent on sentiments, emotions, ideas, standards, ideals, etc., our joy should be unconditional, unasked for, and underserved.

This is because a person's feelings, sentiments, and held ideas are directly influenced and dependent on their level of pleasure. A person is cheerful when in good emotional health, and vice versa. We must be entirely in charge of our emotions to shape our lifestyle in the way we choose. Otherwise, our feelings will start taking over our minds and determine our happiness and sadness.

Unsolicited:

Unlike the solicited way of having peace of mind intentionally, the unsolicited way simply shows having peace of mind unintentionally and without any prior understanding. This is done when an individual inadvertently finds a place, person, or thing that gives that person peace of mind. In several instances, we encounter an event, place, or person we find comfort with. We enjoy being around such people, in a situation, or a place – which happens instantaneously. However, when we tend to leave that place, person, or event – associated with these three elements, we may also lose peace of our mind. Our peace of mind will automatically disappear like it had come to us.

There are a few unsolicited ways of achieving peace of mind. For example, children usually get excited when they see their mother coming from shopping because they expect her to have brought candies or toys for them. Or when kids go home first, they will unintentionally call their mom. That is the reason kids always find inner peace with their moms being around them. Or for some teenagers who play cricket, they automatically feel satisfied when they pass by a cricket ground. This is because they love to play cricket and they enjoy playing cricket. Therefore, seeing a cricket ground unintentionally gives them peace of mind. Even if they notice or not but they will get unsolicited inner peace. To further elaborate on this topic, I have observed several unsolicited ways of achieving peace of mind. They are:

Obsession:

It can occasionally be detrimental to one's mental health to get obsessed with a specific place, location, or person. However, some people are fixated on the good aspects of things that bring them comfort. An activity that one likes performing or establishing goals for oneself and reaching those objectives with all of one's passion are two examples of how a person can generate good energy and positively use the habit of obsession. Many individuals with these features might get obsessed with their objectives to the point that they cannot relax until they have attained their goals; once they have done so, their experience of relief, satisfaction, and excitement increases.

This is why we might have observed that most people with this kind of temperament are always uncomfortable until they achieve what they are obsessed with. Their time will only pass smoothly once they reach the desired objectives. However, as I mentioned, the behavior could also be positive in that obsession is with the things that help a person develop their personality or allow him in some other way.

On the other hand, a sizable portion of young people nowadays are obsessed with achieving virtual popularity. These people are anxious to gain more likes, comments, and followers on social media because having a lot of those things offers them a sense of inner peace. Since people start to think of themselves as social media superstars, the more followers, comments, and likes they receive, the more content they begin to feel within.

It's essential to set goals for yourself and work towards them. Still, it's also vital to prioritize your mental well-being along the way. Sometimes we can become so focused on our objectives that we forget to care for ourselves, leading to unnecessary stress and anxiety. Remember to take breaks and reflect on your needs and emotions. It's okay to feel anxious sometimes, but finding a healthy balance and prioritizing your mental health is crucial.

Being aware that tying your happiness to achieving specific goals can damage your mental health and overall well-being is crucial. While accomplishing objectives can provide temporary satisfaction, constantly setting new goals can disrupt our emotional well-being and cause us inner suffering. It is imperative to cultivate contentment and inner peace that is not reliant on external factors such as goals or specific individuals, locations, or objects. Prioritizing self-care and mental health can aid in developing a healthier mindset and promoting long-lasting happiness.

Therefore, the ability to be at peace should be unconditional and ubiquitous. Otherwise, we would lose control over our happiness if we became preoccupied with finding inner peace based on fulfilling our desires. Once our desires are satisfied, we will experience intense pleasure for some time. Until that time, we may be less likely to be able to be at peace. Consequently, we will begin to yearn to satisfy new desires after a while. If those newly built specific desires are not satisfied, we will continue to feel upset because we will wait for the precise time when our objectives will be met, and our desires will be fulfilled. This saga is going to continue for a long time until a certain point wherein we realize that our mental peace should be unconditional and not stick to our desires. There should be no benchmarks or conditions for our inner peace and happiness.

Forced Respect:

There are many diverse cultural traditions around the globe, each with its standards and laws. However, these cultural standards have limitations in various situations, especially regarding their relevance in the contemporary setting. For instance, in Afghanistan and some parts of Pakistan many people live according to established rules based on the totalitarian form of local leadership with centralized power. As a result, these standards do not apply to the current period, Industry 4.0. Because everyone in today's world, regardless of age, can distinguish between good and evil and make their own decisions. It is likely that those rules were applicable at that certain time when first formulated and followed.

In Afghanistan, where many families still adhere to these standards, the hierarchical structure of the leadership is such that every family has a single head who serves as the only commander or, simply, the family's ruler. Therefore, regardless of whether the head member's instructions are good or bad or whether any family member likes or dislikes the rules, everyone must follow them. But everyone in the family is required to do so.

The fact that most of the families abide by their head's regulations makes the head feel influential and respected. To be sure, there must be someone in those households who never wants to follow such laws. However, that person must be compelled to do so because this is more of a forced respect shown by family members. It is necessary to follow the head's instructions for various reasons. For instance, the family members never seek to offend the elders by going against cultural norms or the beliefs that had been followed by their ancestors.

Since I have developed my exposure to the cultures of Afghanistan in real life, most of my examples are drawn from incidents that occurred there. I noticed one of my neighbors and immediately thought of the phrase "forced respect." Let me narrate here his story, which will help better illustrate the concept. When I was a kid, a boy who lived in my neighborhood was younger than me. That boy also belonged to a family that had a totalitarian form of leadership, which was a constant source of anxiety for him. Even though more than half of his family members were well educated. The boy said that he continued to exhibit conduct that constituted mental bullying.

I can still remember some of his stories since we were both opponents and friends at the same time while playing marbles and flying kites. While playing marbles and flying kites together in his home, we frequently shared our tales. I understood the boy's emotions through his family members' actions. He often turned down my requests to play with me. This was due to his family's harsh treatment that often made him feel mentally unwell. Because their baneful way of life affected him severely that he would frequently isolate himself and refuse to play for periods of time. I began to ponder about the circumstances in his home and other homes in the neighborhood due to the taunting situation that he was experiencing. This made me understand that regrettably, there was little distinction between his family life and other families—including mine—and many others.

The boy's disdain for being treated like a slave and as a tool for forced respect were the leading causes of his mental turmoil. Considering that his elders would force him to perform any duty for them while expecting him to live according to their expectations. When he refused, the elders emotionally stigmatized him. They accused him of disrespecting the family codes and disobeying values. In addition, the boy would complain to me about how his elders occasionally would do something wrong. Then they would blame him since he was the youngest in his family and had no experience addressing the problems he faced.

He failed to express his concerns well, which made it difficult for him to convince others that his elders, rather not himself, were the real culprits. Since he was still a little lad and no one was ready to believe that his elders would ever do something terrible, no one would accept his words. This is because he was a young boy and, on the

THE DEATH WITHIN

other hand, were his elders. Therefore, nobody would believe that the teenage kid could be right, and his elders, that were in the majority, would be wrong. As a result, the boy was the one who received the blame, which made him even more emotionally distressed.

During those times, I learned that every elder in our community—and I am sure in every Afghan community—was obsessed with earning the respect of the younger generation. This respect is ludicrous since kids coerced into showing respect to adults may not be psychologically capable of doing so or complying with the rules being placed on them forcefully. And when a child is made to show respect and follow the elders' instructions, hate grows in that child's heart and mind. When a child begins to view those adults as his foes due to this animosity, the family home will become a jail.

Understanding the mentalities of the family's young members is essential to foster an environment of mutual respect and understanding. An atmosphere where both kids and elders feel valued and respected—and satisfied. Isaac Newton's third law of motion, which states that "every action has an equal but opposite reaction," is what this entire situation makes me think of. Like elders should be respected, children should be treated with kindness and tenderness. Both, therefore, be respected.

However, suppose the chain of respect between teenagers and elders fails. In that case, the youngsters will have several long-lasting mental problems, with depression being one of the most frequent of these problems. These kids will feel depressed and develop long-lasting animosities against their kinfolk, especially the elderly. Teenagers are likely to engage in several other unwanted behaviors that might have severe repercussions and be challenging to make up for.

Teenagers may undergo a significant shift in their behavior and attitude that may impact their personalities for the rest of their lives. For instance, many youths are stigmatized as antisocial or introverted; however, given how outspoken and sociable those teens might have been in the past. However, perhaps their elders' behavior hurt their personalities. I also emphasize that explicit and genuine rejection and hatred are better than coerced and mandatory admiration and respect.

The Lack of Inner Peace

MY THOUGHTS AND personal experience suggest that inner peace is the foundation of a person's general picture of a happy life. The only objective of human beings in their existence on earth should be fixated to find inner peace to possess a happy life. So, people use several approaches to achieve the goal of being happy within. Depending on a person's personality and attitude, spiritual and materialistic techniques may be used to gain inner peace. However, I choose the former since spirituality leads to long-lasting inner peace, and materialism delivers ephemeral peace. Because being spiritual always leads to building a close relationship between a human and the heavenly power (God) with no materialistic expectations and desires.

With spirituality, a person will become disinterested in materialism once a connection with divine power has been established. When people quit being interested in materialism, they start to appreciate what they already have, decreasing their desire for more materialistic possessions. In this approach, a person's desire to have fancy stuff like a luxurious car, fortune, house, etc., decreases. He begins to appreciate the benefits of things God has given him, such as breathing, drinking water, and eating the available food. Thus, he tries to be grateful and satisfied with whatever he already has.

For a good life, humans require mental satisfaction and inner peace as they need food and water. While there are a variety of approaches for humans to find inner peace, there are also several other factors that preclude humans' path toward inner peace. The significance of inner peace is such that a person can also obtain physical well-being by having a keen sense of inner peace. Thus, I describe inner peace as a source of physical vitality and satisfaction—dependent on mental and emotional relaxation. Because inner peace, as mentioned above, results in a person's outer contentment or physiological happiness. Ultimately, this entire phenomenon results in a perfect life—by which I mean a satisfying life.

As mentioned above, several things may prevent people from having inner peace. However, based on my observations, I have found that the most adopted behavioral factors (figure 2) include emotional reaction, the desire to achieve ambitions, an authoritarian attitude, and the dread of future uncertainty. There must be many other factors that might be hazardous to mental peace and inner happiness. However, from what I have observed and experienced, I have finally discovered the factors that are majorly harmful to inner peace.

Our intelligence and mental peace are at risk when we respond emotionally to everything we encounter. Based on the factors mentioned above, having desires is a great habit. Still, it may often double our aspirations, disrupting our inner peace. Because it is a common human nature that once a man achieves something, he desires additional. Regarding utilitarianism, some people naturally possess the feeling of leadership and behave in that capacity in all circumstances.

Although this behavior may benefit the individual himself, it may be detrimental to others' inner peace since this may make them feel constrained. Last but not least, we undoubtedly think uncomfortably worrying about unforeseeable future catastrophes. This is because we would consider both extraordinary and terrible situations that could or might not occur, but thinking about such events will undoubtedly disturb our inner peace. Nonetheless, based on various perspectives of people, inner peace can also be harmed by several other circumstances. The following are a few of the factors I discovered while randomly surveying and observing thirty teenagers in my neighborhood.

THE LACK OF INNER PEACE

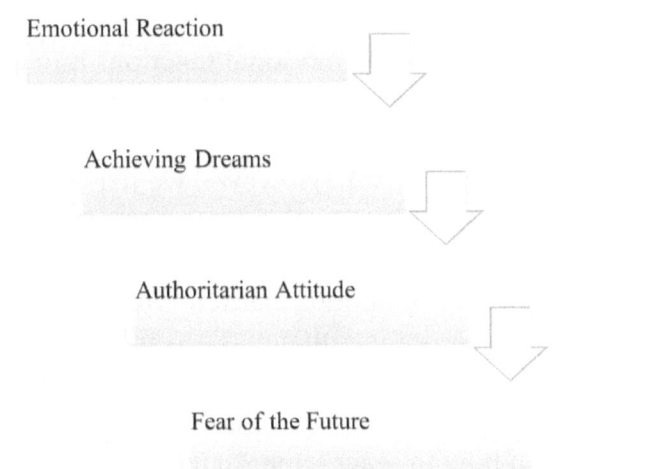

Figure 2. Factors that lead to the lack of inner peace

Emotional Reaction:

Inner peace could be directly or indirectly connected with emotions. The soundness and flimsiness of inner peace are the two common traits. These traits are sometimes naturally built-in and sometimes created based on how a man potentially controls his emotions. Multiple emotional ways affect a person's mental health and inner peace. Among those ways is the emotional reaction, which is vital to deal with – especially during a critical situation wherein a person gets emotionally challenged. Therefore, during a crucial case, a person finds it difficult to control and change his emotions. For instance, a person may react emotionally to a sensitive situation – or a situation that is entirely unexpected and unwanted to that person.

While reacting with emotions, a person may lose consciousness and end up hurting themself. Because emotionally reacting to everything we face will only harm us by preventing us from thinking and acting rationally and calmly. Another reason could be that emotional reaction is always coupled with anger and frustration. While the offense is dangerous to mental peace, intellect, and wisdom, an emotional response associated with frustration would be even more miserable to a person's inner peace.

Since it is evident that emotional reactions hurt a person internally as they come from the heart rather than the mind, they must be avoided. This behavior may impact not just one's inner peace but also one's mental health. However, we may prevent emotional reactions to unfavorable situations by controlling our emotions, which is also a sign of a strong mentality. But the primary question is how to manage our emotions, particularly when they are severely strained by circumstances that make us frustrated. The answer to this question is that we can handle our feelings by depending on our intelligence and knowledge and allowing the brain to choose what to do and how to react rather than the heart. For those prone to anger, it may be challenging for them to contain their feelings of frustration.

However, these individuals eventually need to alter their habits and develop the mental discipline to reason through who, what, and how they should talk before responding to a situation, person, or thing. Since most of the time, when we say something, we realize we should not have said it. Because once we say anything, it is impossible to take it back, which might have disastrous results. For instance, sometimes we say things to people that seem simple initially but might profoundly impact how those people perceive us and their entire lives. However, saying positive words will significantly affect how other people see us. But if we say anything negative, it will affect their behavior towards us in a negative way.

I firmly believe in using reason and thoughtfulness before speaking or taking action. The impact of our words or actions on someone's life and outlook can be challenging to predict. Various factors can trigger emotional reactions, including emotional blackmail, which can manifest in different ways, such as cultural or religious norms. In some of the developing nations in Asia, deeply ingrained superstitious beliefs are still regarded as sacred obligations. They can exert a profound emotional influence on people.

THE LACK OF INNER PEACE

It is common for humans to hold strong beliefs and adhere to certain norms, often believing that failure to follow or respect them will result in consequences in this life and the hereafter, even potentially facing the death penalty. This belief often leads individuals to exploit these norms to accomplish tasks, using the threat of catastrophe if their demands are unmet. Unfortunately, this phenomenon targets younger individuals, particularly those more open-minded and willing to question the status quo. These individuals are often more susceptible to emotional manipulation through norms and values, as they are more likely to critically analyze and challenge them.

Fundamentally, a person's profound faith in social standards and superstitious beliefs is why emotional extortion frequently succeeds. Firm believers in superstitious beliefs or social norms are more susceptible to emotional extortion. For instance, if any of my friends balks at helping me with anything he finds annoying or challenging, I will indirectly or negatively encourage him by telling him that he is not a brave and faithful friend. By appealing to his emotions, I will make him feel proud of being my loyal and courageous friend by asking him to do something to prove it. I will utilize social norms and cultural codes to emotionally blackmail him for doing what I expect of him. Since the Pashtuns are known for maintaining lasting friendships and devotion, which has to do with cultural conventions. Everyone strives to uphold these norms by being trustworthy and keeping friendships, regardless of the aftermath.

Hence, not everyone may constantly act in a way that demonstrates genuine loyalty and friendship maintenance. Those unwilling to maintain a friendship for an extended period may exist for several reasons. However, in my example, I will encourage my friend to agree to my request for help by citing mainstream social norms. As a result, my friend will be driven to try to demonstrate his commitment to being a brave and loyal friend to me. He will accept my request, regardless of how challenging it is for him to help me - or whether he is psychologically capable of doing so - if only to uphold social norms by demonstrating his loyalty and truthfulness.

No matter how grave the consequences of getting a task done by emotionally extorting someone. Using societal norms or anything related to sentiments will make people do anything by being emotionally extorted. Nonetheless, the first aftermath will be an enduring envy created in the heart of those squeezed for the one who emotionally exacts others. Second, the self-respect of that person in the heart of others vanishes. Third, fewer people will trust that person. These are the critical consequences for someone who exploits others' emotions to get his work done.

On the other hand, the same is the case with the one who gets emotionally extorted. The consequences for that person are also severe. He will suffer from mental disturbance anytime he recalls the moment when his emotions were misused, and the trust he had put in was broken. Emotional reaction merely hurts one's feelings rather than the body and can sometimes lead to a fundamental problem.

Often, reacting emotionally can even cause long-term harm to mental health. Suppose a person does not like being surrounded by certain people. Still, he usually gets a chance to come across such people. Thus, whatever the person does or says, he will react emotionally. He pressurizes his emotions and feelings, and then his mind, instead of thinking coherently, starts thinking about those people all the time. That person tries to control his mind and causes him to endure mental pain without doing anything wrong. This practice eventually results in the victim's inner peace being destroyed in several ways such as playing the victim.

a. Playing the Victim:

Most kids with sensitive temperaments will play the victim to prevent harming others verbally or physically. We are trying to deceive ourselves if we believe that by playing the victim, we can act innocent and demand justice from those around us. We have no clue how potentially hazardous our surroundings seem to be. The answer is that nobody is concerned with our inner peace and that whatever happens inside our bodies is invisible to others. It is us who actually bear the brunt of inner suffering.

The only ones who can genuinely comprehend what is happening inside our bodies are us. Only we will be responsible for dealing with the issues and suffering. As a result, I advise against behaving like a victim and instead encourage self-care to achieve inner peace. Here, my objective is to safeguard ourselves from other people's damage rather than oppress them. We suffer more when we act like victims, and society may take advantage of this by exploiting us. It is just like that. We occasionally harm our inner peace to please others. Hurting oneself to please others is never right because we hurt ourselves when we try to please others.

Achieving Dreams:
"The future belongs to those who believe in the beauty of their dreams." – Eleanor Roosevelt

My subjective argument about the above proverb is that it only applies to those from economically well-off families, where the pursuit of individual satisfaction and inner peace take precedence over all other considerations, including societal standards. The above saying has turned out to be inapplicable in the cases of numerous other youngsters, too. For instance, some teenagers come from middle-class households with a life full of hardships and unfulfilled dreams. It is a complex reality for those teens to live with hopes of obtaining their targeted dreams.

A youngster from a household with greater emphasis on cultural values, traditions, and social conventions may also experience a hard life. Teenagers from those middle-class families yearn for a life similar to that of other teens from wealthy families. Middle-class teens' inner peace is not the only thing affected by this; their parents' behavior in urging their children to do as expected is also a reason. The parents are occasionally not even concerned with the aspirations and desires of their children in this regard. Nonetheless, the inner happiness of children is more important than the opinions of other people, even if those opinions may be correct in their perspectives.

To imply the harm done to one's inner peace and state of mind by pursuing one's desires and objectives. Let me share a story I heard from an Afghan roommate while attending college in India. My hostel roommate once said that he had a friend when he was young who was so mature despite being from a poor family. The reason I am writing this story here is to better demonstrate the problem I stated above. My roommate said that his neighboring friend was a good and pretty intelligent boy. He was tremendously committed to pursuing a prosperous professional career.

Thus, he desired to finish his studies, obtain a master's degree in the field of his choice, and then land the ideal job. After achieving his career goals, he then intended to consider marriage and other aspects of his life. His parents, though, were firmly in the opposing camp. They had already planned to set up their son's engagement with a close family friend's daughter while he was still pursuing his studies. My roommate's friend's father had promised the girl's family when the girl and the boy were still toddlers that both the kids would marry when they become mature.

My roommate's friend was young enough to fulfill his parents' goal, which was no more complicated than agreeing to marry that girl, but his parents pushed him to marry, nonetheless. His parents only wanted their son to wed that girl, as his parents would frequently admit, because of the friendship and long-standing relationship between the girl's family and the family of my roommate's friend. It appeared difficult for my roommate's friend to decline his parents' decision. Given that this was a genuine oath between two mutually oriented friends who strongly believed in societal norms, it was not just a promise.

Yet my roommate's friend intimated that if he were to accept his parents' choice, he might have to give up on his career aspirations. He was not mentally ready for marriage since he was so focused on advancing his career and was preoccupied with reaching his goals. He was not only concerned about the additional responsibility and burden at that young age, which he believed would be a barrier in the way of his professional aspirations. At such an early age, he thought it was a big challenge to manage both his married life and his professional career simultaneously.

My roommate usually got dismayed and downcast while talking to me about his friend's problems since he had been trapped in a pickle. And he could see that the predicament would drain him of the peace he had come to associate with, hailing from a middle-class household and pursuing his dreams. At such an early age, he would argue that balancing his career goals and the family's needs was challenging. I could only empathize with him as I listened to his friend's story, and I still empathize now that those events are in my memory, especially the mental disturbance that my roommate's friend experienced.

Because of the pain the boy suffered, I felt terrible for him and sympathized with my roommate about his friend's predicament. On the other hand, I noticed my roommate's face had gone pale one day. I questioned him about what had happened straight away. After a while of silence, he eventually admitted that his friend had to give in to his parents' wishes and had engaged the girl. After several months, he finally tied a permanent knot with that girl and eventually both married. That young boy, around 16 years old, was highly impressionable. In the initial stages of his marriage, my roommate's friend was content and delighted with his new life, as my roommate would later say. Unfortunately, things started to go awry and worsened with his married life after a few months. He began to complain about his routine and the behavior of his wife in particular.

Even yet, I was still interested in how that boy had altered his perspective to compromise on his ambitions since I knew how hard it might have been for him to balance his married life and his aspirations. But my roommate clarified my confusion by stating that his friend thought his wife was a very mature and kind girl. But after a few weeks, his wife started behaving differently. Due to his busy schedule of academics and other vital duties that he would do to reach his goals, his wife would get less time to spend with him. The boy first believed that his wife understood his circumstances and would help him reach his ambitions, but subsequently realized that she had become impatient and craved her husband's company.

Based on what my roommate would say about his friend's marriage, I concluded that, in addition to the duties, there were misunderstandings and differences in the mentalities and levels of understanding between my roommate's friend and his wife. As usual, his professional and personal aspirations had preoccupied my roommate's friend. On the other side, his wife was obsessed with him, always seeking his attention and, more crucially, his willingness to compliment and laud her attractiveness, even if she did not behave well. Her actions would distract the boy's attention and disturb his mental health. He constantly expressed disappointment and pessimism in response to his wife's actions.

I discovered that he was correct in his decision to forego marriage at that age and during such a delicate time after seeing his married life. I believe that people in such communities should realize that marriage is a natural and inevitable component of life which will happen at some time in everyone's life, whether they want it or not. The same might have been true about that boy; he could have wed later in life, and that too to a girl who shared his level of maturity and understanding and effective communication skills. He could give the girl ample time and love her even if she did not have his level of maturity because he would have already accomplished nearly all, if not all, of his professional goals at that point.

Given the boy's age, his parents should have placed more importance on his work, life objectives, and, most importantly, mental health than marriage. Because one can arrange marriage at any stage of life as it is a basic necessity. Yet after one reaches a certain point, pursuing a career becomes much more challenging, which may not always be the case since some people can continue working after marriage. Due to their partners' cooperation and understanding, this is a rare instance. They may also have alternative sources of income, so it might not be a problem for them to prioritize marriage over career. Hence, it was crucial for the boy's and his wife's mental health.

Nevertheless, it would have been better if he had been allowed to choose the girl he wanted to marry. Unfortunately, the family of my roommate's friend did not view marriage as a decision based on mutual agreement. Instead, his parents were only forcing it due to their personal issues. A better option would have been to find a girl who could understand him. Someone who could read his mind and emotions even if he said nothing at all. A girl who shared his objectives, sense of happiness, attitude, mentality, personality, and level of comprehension. Someone who would place his mental well-being before attempting to force him to pay attention. And lastly, someone who could empathize with him in any circumstance.

My roommate would become quite dejected and upset when he related the story of his friend to me since he felt as though he was going through this difficulty himself. My roommate kept asserting that his friend's family had taken his aspirations away from his friend because of emotional pressure. Even though, as my roommate would remark, his friend had started to deal with a mental issue and various other challenges concerning his career.

The situation had unfortunately turned static, despite his tears, sadness, and lamentations. Later, even his parents had realized that their son was true to pursue his ambitions rather than settle down and marry. On this, I would explain to my roommate that according to his friend's story, his aspirations damaged his happiness. But later, I would contemplate and tell myself that it was the decision of the boy's parents and the importance they had placed on the relationship with the girl's family which damaged the boy's happiness.

Belonging to a middle-class family, if I were that boy, I would either continue to follow the same old customs or refrain from setting myself any new aspirations – to go with the societal flow. Or I could vehemently disagree with the dominant status quo and standards and put my inner happiness first. And I would decide against getting married at that moment. Alternatively, I would focus more on achieving my professional goals. But the issue is whether my parents would still consider me a decent son and if their relationship with the girl's family would have remained intact if I had disobeyed their choice in that instance.

To respond to this question, the consequences of that boy's

troubled relationship with the girl were worse than the brokering of their families' relationship. Because the inner peace, satisfaction, agreement, and mutual understanding of the boy and his wife were more important than the mainstream promises of their parents. Meanwhile, the boy's career goals were equally crucial as his parent's decision, based on which they tried upholding their commitment to the girl's family.

Authoritarian Attitude:

Management is a universal concept, according to renowned organizational theorists Koontz and O' Donell. This means that management is prevalent everywhere, whether it be in a family, a corporate office, a school, a university, a college, a religious institution, an army training base, a sports team, a district administration, a village administration, a county administration, a state administration, ministries, a parliament, upper and lower houses, or a provincial administration. As a result, every management style is unique and pertinent to that particular place, from a small household to a nation's whole government structure.

People at the top, including professionals and lawyers, design the various management principles per the demands of a particular institution and level of authority, or sometimes the codes have been passed down through a lineage in the form of an ongoing succession. Only some time management techniques work and are liked by people in every context. Many people, however, might not consider certain management styles that they live under to be productive and beneficial, depending on their specific parameters and viewpoint.

Nonetheless, a management style might also be disruptive to a person's inner peace in addition to many other unwanted aspects. As a result of my observations and experiences in the real world, I have realized that the primary cause of internal suffering for teenagers in a family or subordinates in an organization may be the authoritarian-based management style of the superior or the leadership of a family or an organization.

For instance, a teenager may prefer something other than the managerial approach in his household. An employee's work performance may deteriorate if he cannot work happily. The observance of norms in families and societies may not make some people content. While others might need to be more content with the institution's structure, they attend for their education. Such discontentment might disturb their inner peace. Additionally, a person's inability to challenge, alter, or oppose the norms doubles the degree of such misery.

A subordinate, for example, working at the very bottom of the organizational hierarchy who dislikes the rules that he cannot alter or defy may experience severe mental anguish. Such instances frequently occur in organizations with authoritarianism or a centralized form of leadership where the power is concentrated in the grasp of a single individual. Similarly, we often find children and teenagers in families who disagree with the beliefs or traditions their families uphold. Most often, this occurs in households with an autocratic management approach, similar to the organizations mentioned above. The reason is that teenagers in those families are prevented from speaking openly, expressing their emotions, and having their views and voices heard.

This may be because, in many places like Afghanistan, it is regarded as disrespectful to elders when teenagers talk candidly or unapologetically about their emotions – especially in front of their elders. According to their conventional values, it is believed that it is unethical for teenagers to express themselves so openly in front of their parents and elders. Mainly because when their elders talk, teenagers are expected to remain silent in their presence. On the contrary, those teenagers grow accustomed to the belief that by keeping quiet in front of their elders, they will demonstrate their loyalty to the predominant belief system and respect for their elders.

This rooted belief thus motivates teenagers to follow conventional norms irrespective of how they may affect their inner peace and overall personality and disposition. However, teenagers may not show respect or do the traditional standards any favors by indulging in such behavior. They only harm their inner peace and mold their personalities to fit the expectations of their elders and fit with society, which is what happens. Their personalities, however, are shaped to give the elders a short-term egoistic euphoria while sacrificing their long-term mental peace by acting contrary to how teenagers should behave to be mentally at peace.

Teenagers living under an authoritarian form of leadership find themselves less worthy and mentally suppressed. As a result, they begin to feel isolated and emotionally detached from their families as they are sidelined by not having their voices heard and their feelings respected. This behavior of such teenagers also leads to the fact that they build hatred against their family members for their utilitarian behavior. The teenagers feel that their family members neither love them nor value them.

Other elders or the head of the family responsible for looking after the family believe that they may lose control of the family's leadership if they do not centralize the authority of running the family. Thus, everyone in the family will start defying both the head's rules and commands and the codes of their ancestors that they have been living on. In many instances, the intention of the head of the family to limit the power solely to himself is correct.

This may be because he might have witnessed any bad behavior in society that he thinks will also affect his family members – especially the younger ones. Per the head, that could entice a decentralized form of management in the family, and every family member will thus decide independently. As a result, anarchy will ensue in the family. Therefore, the head does not want those societal substandard to negatively affect the teenagers and other members of his family. Eventually, he tries to keep every family member, especially the teenagers, under rigorous control. Nevertheless, he forgets that he can alternatively use soft approaches of grasping control over his family members to protect them from being inflicted by society's inadequate norms.

Families that are prosperous and happy have structures that are similar to those of many other successful organizations. For instance, many corporate organizations follow a strategic style of management, where everyone is offered the opportunity to express themselves and does so without any hesitation. As their voices are heard, and their opinions are respected, employees in these organizations feel respected and treasured. As a result, those employees start to feel motivated and create a sense of attachment to the organization they work for. Additionally, they are satisfied and joyful.

They will, therefore, always aspire to do their best and honestly do their job. However, failing organizations take a different approach to motivating staff members and considering their satisfaction. Such organizations, for instance, consider the concept of "human resource" literally as it is by treating humans as resources. In those companies, superiors treat their employees more like resources than humans. They prioritize their profits while giving the slightest consideration to the happiness and mental health of their employees. As a result, the workers feel cut off from the company, and their productivity rapidly declines. Eventually, the supervisors either warn the employee or fire them after noticing their ineffective job performance.

As a result, the company and the individual will primarily feel the consequences. The individual will lose his job. There may not be any other means of support, and he could start to experience depression due to his joblessness. He will also have to deal with the anxiety over supporting his family, paying the expenses, and making up for the gap that prevents him from pursuing a job in his field. On the other side, the company will lose a worker, human capital, and an asset that was significant to some of the work in the company.

The recruiting process for a new employee must once more be started by the human resources department. The fired employee's job will be shunned or assigned to someone else until that time, which will strain the company. Due to this, corporates, and specifically the human resources departments within them, should regard their employees as assets and pillars of their organizations rather than as mere resources.

Therefore, motivation and a strategic leadership style are the best approaches to living in a family, like the frameworks of many significant firms and organizations. Every member living under a strategic framework in households is motivated and content. Because the opinions of all individuals in the family are valued. However, if family leaders were educated, they could apply the concepts of Maslow's theory of motivation, which states that an employee receives both what he deserves and needs. Most significantly, per Maslow's theory, an employee gets fulfillment of both their psychological and physiological requirements. The same holds for families, depressed ones, where there are occasional disputes and disagreements between family members.

Commonly in these lineages, the primary cause is the family's authoritarian management structure, which frequently harms the mental health of its members, particularly the younger ones. The generational gap may be a significant factor, resulting in differences between older and younger groups' mindsets. The elderly members in those households believe they should be regarded imperially due to generational differences in perception. The younger ones, however, have very distinct viewpoints. How they are treated, and act should be equal to how their elders are treated. The teenagers think that if youngsters are treated leniently, they will be more likely to behave with the elders with great reverence.

Nonetheless, most of the time, the older members of those families consider it a dishonor to be treated in a similar fold as are treated the young members. In families where social taboo prevails widely, it is difficult for the young members to challenge such mainstream beliefs. Because driven by their authoritarian attitude, elders are obsessed with their royal status given by societal views and culturally accepted codes. This is why such a utilitarian-based mindset of the elderly often leads to a conflict of interest and internal disputes among family members – or often results in remorse and taunting ramifications.

For instance, following the story of my roommate's friend in the previous section, his story reflects the authoritarian attitude of his parents. Among other reasons, his parents' imperial mindset did not allow him to defy their decision – simply because the societal taboo gives the older members of families a sense of psychological authority. These members then exploit their power – disguised as holy cultural codes or sometimes connoted as religious principles. But such a phenomenon, if misused, most often does away with the inner peace of the young members of a family. Also, do away with their dreams, personality, mental health, and whole life.

As a result, the teenagers realize they do not deserve anything. The reason is already mentioned in the preceding section. Eventually, teenagers begin to think in society they must follow what has been followed by their elders and their ancestors for decades and centuries. If otherwise not, they face the consequences. The consequences may be detachment from their loved ones, or they may get discharged from the property. Therefore, they fear their life being pushed into a consequential fate if they fail to adhere to the societal codes. They also fear losses in this world and the hereafter as per superstitious beliefs disguised as religious norms or cultural principles.

This is because these teenagers are warned that if they defy the cultural or mainstream principles, God may be unhappy with them for their deeds and throw them to hell fire. Therefore, afraid of such imaginary and real-life miseries, the personality of such youngsters drowns, their interpersonal skills vanish, and their communication skills and self-esteem disappear. They are kept in a situation wherein their thinking and analytical abilities are confined. They think only their socially accepted achievements are to be lauded by the elderly members of their families. Because societal beliefs do not allow them to think out of the box – and analyze things using their logic. Also, their minds are limited to fulfilling the basic needs and societal codes, which makes them engaged with trivial things such as adhering to mainstream beliefs.

This was also one of the primary reasons why my roommate's friend did not use logic or argue with his parents to defend his life, inner peace, and dreams. However, he was not blamed, as he had lost the ability to reason, argue, and debate due to severe mental pressure. His freedom was taken away under the umbrella of the societal taboo. Therefore, for the rest of their lives, many such youngsters are compelled to follow the societal beliefs and codes left over in perpetual succession.

Fear of the Future:

The inner peace of humans, particularly teenagers, can be diminished by thinking about uncertainty. Uncertainty can lead a person to think about both positive and negative results since, commonly, two outcomes will happen in the future. A person's mental health is impacted by future uncertainty because thinking about fate causes them to focus on the worst-case scenarios rather than the best-case scenarios. A lot of the time, this type of behavior causes humans to overthink and consider all outcomes, even negative ones. It is also understood that pondering too much disturbs our peaceful mind. Attributed to the fact that when we force our thoughts to think, we tend to think about things that are pointless and may never occur but that will harm our mental health.

On the contrary, most teenagers appreciate and enjoy their life without fully understanding things until they enter their adulthood stage. As they approach adulthood or just before maturity, they consider their future and fret about their uncertain fate. While most teenagers continue their high school education during that period. They particularly need their friends' and family members' mental and spiritual support. Sadly, many teenagers at this crucial juncture of life do not receive the necessary psychological and spiritual care from their friends and families. This could be for a variety of reasons, including the fact that they come from middle-class families where the focus is somewhere else, their ingrained moral code is different and focuses on other aspects of life, or the family's hierarchy approach is utilitarian and giving less consideration to kids and many more. These may be the factors that preclude the way for friends or family members from adequately taking into account the mental health of teenagers.

Similarly, the failure to make their own decisions is one of the other core factors that cause teenagers to have trouble getting mental peace since they worry about their uncertain future. For instance, after misbehaving, we may have seen children acting scared. Alternatively, a teenager who performs poorly on an exam may experience anxiety due to the unknown future that lies ahead. A child's inability to assess his performance in the present and the past, or to determine how to enhance his abilities to perform well in the future is the key driving force behind the lack of mental peace.

These kids, who lack experience, frequently worry that their parents would be displeased with them, that their friends would make fun of them, or that society would stigmatize them for their poor performance in an exam. But in that child's case, the real issue is not a fear of uncertainty; it is a problem of being unable to deal with uncertainty and not being able to make rational decisions to deal with the circumstance at hand and produce solutions for the future. That such children typically rely on their family or friends during decision-making poses another question in this context. The family members make decisions about those children's current and future. Their mental strength and inner selves are entirely out of their control. Mainly because their parents, other members of their family, and occasionally their friends' control both their mental and bodily behavior.

It concludes that the incapacity to take charge of their life and a lack of self-reliance are the two main reasons teenagers see the prospect of their future as more dreadful. That, as a result, causes them mental anguish through overthinking. On the other side, we may have seen many other teenagers who are more interested in the present than the future and tend to prefer their happiness over other things. They are more likely to live freely in the present moment and make autonomous decisions if we pay close attention to those types of teens. They do not care if their friends or family members complain or become upset with them. Their pleasure and inner peace are what they are concerned about. Unlike many ordinary kids, they are free from the memories of their past lives. The present is all that matters to them, not the past or the future. They simply ignore whatever occurs to them and move on with their lives.

The drawback of such reckless behavior is that it reveals a lack of genuine understanding of life's purpose in these young people. They simply follow a regimen. They take no action for their welfare and the well-being of others. Considering how much they like living their ordinary lives. Because they are overly concerned about their personal life, they rarely find time to think about other human beings and make a positive impact on other people's lives. This is the primary reason their existence has no significance for people. For others, their presence or absence has no bearing. Given that these individuals are unconcerned with the future, nothing can cause them to lose their peace of mind about the future.

The past has imprisoned some people, on the other hand, which causes them to worry more about their future and harms them in the present. Their thoughts are forced to continue living with the memories of the past even though they are physically living in the present. Sadly, lingering on the past only encourages overthinking, one of the leading causes of mental suffering. Living with memories does not give any benefits other than mental anguish. People's memories can keep them bound in their minds for various causes. This is based on two possibilities: either their previous life was peaceful and happier than the present or darker and more depressing.

In the case of a happier past, people frequently reflect on their pleasant memories and try to use those pleasant memories to calm themselves during their present unpleasant times. On the other hand, people with a more complicated past tend to reflect on how much they have endured and all the adverse incidents that occurred in their history, which eventually hurt them and disturb their peace of mind. People who have experienced traumatic situations in the past frequently reflect on those events and fret that those events will recur in their future lives, which is why they fear for their future. As a result, their present-day inner peace is harmed by such overthinking behavior.

However, instead of worrying about whether or not unpleasant events of the past might recur in the future, people should try to learn from those bad events and be well-prepared to either confront them head-on or effectively prevent them from happening. I say this because once we consider our previous experiences as lessons to learn, no matter how negative they were in the past, we will continue to notice significant modifications in our level of thinking and the way we perceive every experience of life. We will perceive every experience optimistically and strive to mature by learning from each one. We may even consider negative situations positively. Most of the time, life does not have to be happy and positive.

Therefore, we must be prepared for the worst. For this to do, we need to accept the opposite of things. Because everything has two sides to this life on the planet Earth. Therefore, one side without the other is incomplete; the two sides should go hand in hand to complete one another. For instance, a male without a female is imperfect, as is white without black, and so on. We can only understand the significance of one side if we have experienced, observed, or owned the opposing side, so accepting the opposite side of things is essential.

In the same way, going through tough times in life is just as crucial as going through good times. This is because we can more fully understand how significant and lovely an enjoyable time can be after going through tough times. We will be more likely to appreciate living in every moment of life, accept every experience and different aspects of life, and subsequently start to learn from each of them. This is possible when we understand how valuable it is to experience the opposite of the coin.

The Bottom Line:

Every human being's feeling and emotions must be empathized with and respected. Every human being should confine the horizon of their personal, religious, and societal beliefs merely to their private life. Because beliefs are something that has nothing to do with others. Everyone is responsible for their personal way of life. Something suitable for one may not be good for others. Something sacred to one may be of less value to others. Or something applicable in one human's life may not be appropriate in another human's life. Therefore, humans should never impose their personal beliefs on others. Therefore, everyone can decide the good for their life and future. Especially choosing a way that gives them inner peace. Nonetheless, they cannot harm others in exchange for pursuing happiness and inner peace. However, it is acceptable to listen to other people's suggestions and advice with the liberty to decide whether to accept.

When a person is depressed, giving up is not the solution, but the answer is to face the situation and figure out the actual issue. The tendency to ignore or skip stressful situations is also not the solution. However, the key is facing the problem with a strong mindset and perceiving that every bad or good condition is going fleet. The most important thing is to adjust to every situation and adopt the behavior of being flexible. Anything we think is negative is because our mind shapes it negatively, and what we think is positive is portrayed positively by our mind. It is the mindset that perceives things positively and negatively, so if we can control our minds, we can manage any situation.

For example, if an individual facing an analogous situation, like my roommate's friend, is advised to create an atmosphere wherein his partner gets motivated to stand by him. Where the couple reaches a level of mutual understanding. Although anyone in the couple whose personality level is higher than the other may not be ready to step into the story of the other. Therefore, the other person should at least try to uplift his/her standards, mindset, or personality level to match his/her partner. This simply means that both should have a similar perspective and a sense of humor to understand one another. However, both should understand each other, both their silence and words.

Let me conclude the first section by adding the fourth mindfulness principle from Buddha's teachings: Awareness of Suffering: This principle emphasizes humans to understand that awareness of looking deeply at the essence of problems can contribute to our personality development in terms of compassion and finding ways to ride out mental suffering. We, as humans, are not required to ignore or skim over suffering.

This is because to solve a problem, we are supposed to seek ways to stay connected with those who also suffer from the same or similar pain as we do. This way, we will be able to first understand their situation deeply, and then this understanding will help us understand ours and thus turn misery into peace, joy, etc. For such a level of experience, it is vital to refer to books and have a deep relationship with them. This is the reason I would choose books over humans to teach me because, unlike humans, books teach without causing me any damage – mental damage in particular.

SECTION – B.
HOMES PLAY A ROLE

In this section, Families are referred to as "Homes," and families have a considerable influence on the behavior and perception of a teenager toward the outside world. A family may have both positive and negative consequences for a child. For instance, the extent of the communication gap and the level of family understanding among a teenager's family members define such an impact. Therefore, this section discusses how such an impact can damage a teenager's mental health and how that teenager's behavior changes as a byproduct of family members' actions and behavior. To understand the influences of a family's behavior on a child's mental health, I have centered on my observations of friends and other teenagers to base my subjective arguments.

Home is a Prison

WHENEVER A KID is at home, he always feels safe and satisfied. A child always values and likes his mother's caresses, so he views his parents—especially his mother—as benevolent and endearing. Similar to physical dependence on food and shelter, a kid's emotionally inclined mental reliance on his parents increases as they raise him. Because parental emotional support, particularly from the mother, is a child's only source of pleasure and fulfillment. A child's mother's cuddles on her lap are his only solace during that innocent stage of a child's life. As I have already stated, his only source of happiness is his parents' love and mental support. The natural phenomenon of a child's entire birth process, which makes a child attached to his mother, is why a child is more emotionally attached to his mother.

When parents demonstrate affection for their children that the children recognize, which subsequently fosters a solid emotional bond, such emotional support is further strengthened. But if that emotional bond dissolves for some reason, it hurts both the kid and the parents. In addition to parents, other family members are crucial to a child's emotional and psychic well-being. The justification for this is that, like with his parents, a child develops an emotional bond with his siblings and other family members, and based on this psychological bond, he develops expectations and trust. He never feels reluctant to ask his other family members for help, just like he can easily approach his parents for any desired assistance.

Due to the built-in emotional attachment of children to their family members, they enjoy spending every moment of life with their loved ones. Because they feel secure and comfortable with them. We might have observed kids crying when they are kept away from their loved ones – especially moms. Despite getting enough affection and love from other people, those kids never want to stay away from their parents and siblings. Again, the reason is the built-in emotional attachment between a child and his family. Those types of children are overly sensitive and emotionally soft. They tend to remain alongside their parents and family members all the time because the company of their parents and siblings gives them inner peace.

From family gatherings and events to average days, those kids love spending time with their loved ones. They consider their loved ones to be the sole reason for their happiness. Therefore, they also love spending their whole life in their homes with family members. Spend the nights in their bedrooms with deep and relaxing sleep. That sleep becomes more joyful when they spend their day playing tirelessly and return home weary and craving rest. That sleep in their beds after extremely tiring time at a playground is no lesser than a heaven for children. Overall, kids cherish every little thing about their home and family. From endless teasing with siblings and loved ones to the convenience of occasionally eating in home kitchens and using restrooms.

Children also view their rooms, especially their beds, as a unique kind of heaven on earth, and it only grows more wonderful and comfier when their moms are home. No matter how sad or frustrated children may be, the instant their mother holds them in her arms, they feel secure and at ease. We can still retain excellent and lousy childhood experiences as dreams, even as adults. Without a doubt, everyone can relate to this. We only realize how much fun and freedom we had as children once we reached adulthood. This is due to a common trait of human nature: we only recognize something's value once we lose it or see someone else has it. Also, we are not content with the things we now own. We cannot comprehend the actual worth of items, which is the main reason. When we do, we will feel more content. This also relates to our daily lives. The more we learn to value the things we have right now, the less regret we will have over missing them in the future.

For example, during our childhood, we desired to play with various toys, especially those that other children were playing with - the children whose wealthy parents may fulfill their hopes and aspirations. Such children would have access to more expensive playthings. However, I am confident these kids would love playing with their toys less than poor children when they receive one. This is so because wealthy children only know the toys' prices and not their true worth, whereas poor children understand the value of those toys. Poor children see the value of a toy more than its price because they know what it feels like to have and play with it, unlike wealthy children who rarely comprehend the value of things more than the price. Because they afford things, they can only understand the cost. I am sure rich children may only understand their wealth's value once they lose it.

Similarly, people tend to appreciate things more when they are not available to them. Again, many children, especially the impoverished ones, need more fancy clothing, toys, comfortable beds, blankets, or even food. They also occasionally lack friends with whom to joke around and chat. Even worse, they have not felt their parents' love and emotional support and care because most poor children are too busy working, making them child workers or not having families. Such children appreciate their parents' love, their siblings' assistance, and cozy beds for sleeping. I mentioned the lack of parental love for poor children because their parents are busy earning bread for their kids, and rarely do they have time to think about the non-materialistic needs of their children – which are love and emotional support.

However, the solution to this problem is the intention and firm determination of the children to work and change their usual conditions. It is difficult for their parents to do so because they are busy earning bread for the family. Therefore, the children could do so when they become adults. One person should work hard to change the lives of the rest of the family and the next generations. Otherwise, the perpetual succession of poverty will remain static for generations.

Since children are thought to be more avaricious than adults, they prefer to have everything they desire. Because they aspire to live the life of rich kids, which is mostly just a fantasy, impoverished kids' homes are no less than prisons to them. They consider their own lives to be an unfair and biased act of fate. They think it was not their decision to be born into a poor family, but why are their lives not changed even after their families realize their poor condition? These youngsters believe that their way of life cannot be altered. The reason is that the family's breadwinners are mentally bound to do specific things that can hardly support them financially. Or it can be due the societal norms and religious or cultural beliefs. From a spiritual point of view, the idea that poverty is something that God appreciates or that God likes the poor and that; as a result, the poor will be the first to enter paradise before the rich is another reason.

This explains why a poor lifestyle persists for such a long time. This idea is nothing short of absurd, yet it is promoted by many religious masters like Mullahs and other people of influence – especially in Muslim communities. Nevertheless, this pro-poverty attitude is totally at odds with the fundamentals of every religion, including Islam. Because one of the primary elements influencing the creation of many sins and crimes is poverty. For instance, a burglar could steal because he needs money to support his family and himself. Thus, he steals, and if he is caught or questioned, he will start telling lies to cover up his sin and crime of theft. A thief who lies to conceal a crime is guilty of sin. As a result, he is both a thief and a liar. Once more, the critical factor is acceptance of continued poverty. Denying the reality that poverty is the root of all sins and crimes.

Apart from the above discussion, there are several additional explanations for why many children—especially those with feeble minds and hearts—feel like their homes are jails and pressure cookers. As a result, these children mature before their time and before the age at which they should. Such children begin to comprehend the harsh realities of life at a very young age, either strengthening their minds or leaving them wrecked. Use of schoolwork as a means of abusing children to do tasks, for instance, as well as utilizing other emotionally risky methods to coerce children into doing homework or accepting a particular law, such as using threats to deter parents from giving their children pocket money. Adults are unaware of this practice's dangers to their children's developing minds. Unfortunately, this pattern of conduct will persist for a long time in the coming generation—for centuries.

Because this habit has been practiced for millennia and produces mental stress in youth, adults from the present generation must break the chain by altering it. If this does not happen, the next generation will think that forcing children to comply with elders' requests through emotional manipulation is acceptable in culture or even encouraged by religion. Because many of today's so-called cultural and religious norms that still govern the way we live were initially once viewed as acts of injustice committed by the elite class that remained unchallenged and unquestioned. As a result, these moral and ethical guidelines from various religions have come to define much of our way of life. They are often considered to be sacred laws.

In this section, I have argued with the help of the components depicted in Figure 3 to better illustrate the subject matter. Emotional Connection, Self-Esteem, Toxic Parents, and Female's Vulnerability are some of these aspects.

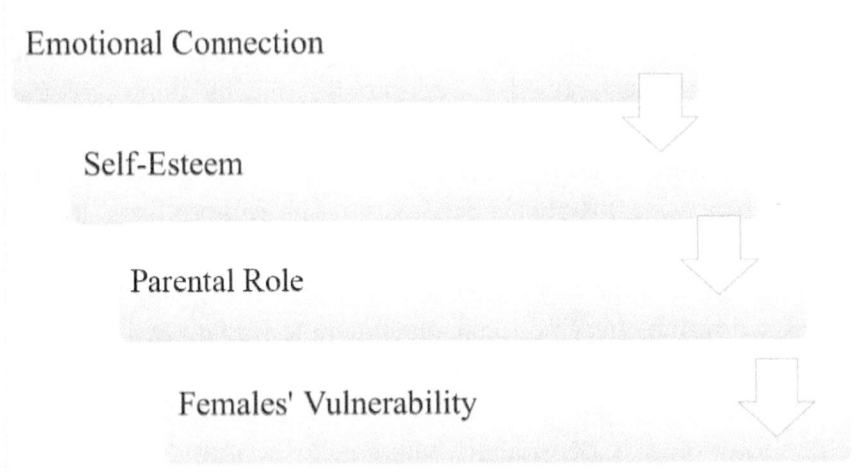

Figure 3. Family behavior that hurdle the inner peace of teens & females

Emotional Connection

FINDING OUT IF a person is emotionally connected to someone, a thing, or a place is always my first and foremost question to ask whenever I see someone, I believe to be experiencing mental distress. The sole purpose of asking this question is to identify whether the person is suffering because of emotional duties or if they are being emotionally restrained and imprisoned. I insist on asking this question since my observations of life have consistently shown that emotional connection is one of the significant barriers to one's happiness and success. Emotional attachment is also a dangerous deterrent to accomplishing one's objectives.

For example, a middle-class boy may not be able to achieve his career goals because he needs to support his family by doing a job that he may or may not like. He may also find it challenging to balance his career and position when he is persistent in pursuing his career while working. However, it is always possible that he is more likely to give up his career dreams by focusing on work, especially to earn money to support his family. The boy's intention to work while giving up on his dreams is driven by his emotional attachment to his family.

Such an emotional connection of a person can be both innate and acquired. This means the emotional bond created with family members by birth is considered inherent. In contrast, an accepted emotional connection is said to be made with friends, peers, or loved ones. Therefore, we often have an emotional relationship with our family members, friends, or the person we love. I call it the emotional connection because we feel for a person with strong emotions and feelings. So much so we simply sympathize with their pain and empathize with their feelings. They are the people we depend on, trust, and expect more than we think. And if that person breaks our trust, we reduce the amount of our dependence and expectations that we have of that person. As a result, we tend to suffer mentally because we cannot prepare for the unexpected – which is the breaking of our trust. Because we mentally suffer due to our mindset being shaped optimistically about the person we trust and depend on.

Conversely, our dependence and expectations are contingent upon the person we trust. If that trust is betrayed, those dependencies and expectations end as well. As a result, we begin to experience emotional suffering. Our sense of familiarity, empathy, and compassion for that person progressively declines due to the anguish we experience when our trust is betrayed. We frequently carry animosity toward the person or simply forget about them. We will feel bad mentally because we are forcing our minds to think about that individual in both situations. The issue is why we must give that person a top priority in our minds by thinking about them nonstop. Why do they control our thoughts? What matters is that we think; whether we think positively or negatively about that individual is meaningless. By thinking about them we let them rule our mind, which alone is enough to harm our mental health.

While it is difficult to ignore and get that person out of our minds, my experience shows that as much as we try to ignore something, we tend to keep that in mind for a long time – which is even worse for our mental peace. On the other hand, our feeling of revenge can be harmful to our mental peace because every time, we will be wasting our energy while waiting for a perfect time to get revenge by harming that person. We build the feeling of revenge because of our egoistic temperament. Our ego motivates us from within to get revenge on the person who breaks our trust and gives us inner pain.

If, on the one side, we accept to follow and satisfy our heart and ego just by taking revenge, but on the other hand, we harm ourselves by having that particular person rule over our mind every time we think of getting revenge. This is because we may either take revenge or not, but we will surely end up harming our inner peace. Therefore, the best way out is to forget and forgive that person and let God take care of the rest. Nonetheless, it is equally essential to ensure that we learn enough lessons from the experience with that person and the inner pain inflicted on us to never let that happen again.

Now that we understand the notion of emotional connection let us get into its concept a little deeper to understand the several ways a person gets hurt due to emotional connection. Emotional connections can be dangerous to one's mental peace in several ways. For instance, there are people to whom we are intricately connected, who cunningly act as if they are helping us. Still, in reality, they are the ones who will hurt us the most. These people can be our close friends, family members, or relatives. One of the standard techniques that these people use is that sometimes due to their envious nature, they will try to push us into trouble in many ways.

For example, these people show the world our lousy image by denigrating our name, disrespecting us, or enticing us to do something wrong and unethical. Suppose we disagree to accept to do what they ask us for. In that case, they start emotionally extorting us with oaths of friendship, relations, etc. As a result, we will get mentally stranded and need clarification between heart and mind. Our hearts might ask us to accept their words, while the mind will force us to deny doing what that person wants us to do.

This vicious fight between the mind and heart will kill our inner peace unless we reach a final decision. However, suppose the person accepts the decision of the mind. In that case, the heart will feel dissatisfied, and this will also result in the relationship of the person getting mentally harmed because a decision that comes from the mind is often logical and beneficial for a person in the long run – but it may harm one's emotionally-linked relationship with the family members or friends and relatives. On the other hand, if a person listens to the heart while making a decision, there will be ramifications because a decision from the heart may lead to short-term happiness and cause a disguised emotional connection to remain unbroken for a long time.

However, if both parties learn about the reality, there may be a prospect of perilous ramifications. I say ramifications because if a person bases his or her decisions on the heart and accepts to sustain an emotional connection, he or she will end up suffering within. This is because humans tend to make decisions listening to their heart basically because that person is emotionally forced while sidelining the mind and thinking logically about the cons of such relationships in the long term.

Most of the time, teenagers withstand the worst emotional connection with their family members in their homes in one way or another. However, in developing nations such as Afghanistan, where societies are less developed, the victims are expected to be often teenagers and female members. This is mainly because of the differences in the mindsets of the teenagers who have grown up either in the nineties or the 21st century post-2000 and the generation born in the seventies and earlier. Also, in the case of the female members of the families, they usually suffer due to the mainstream male-led hierarchical structure and the family's authoritarian leadership style. For instance, women in those societies are given lesser participation in decision-making than they deserve.

This is mainly because women in far-flung regions are either kept less or completely uneducated or spend most of their time within the precinct of their homes. Because of gender-based traits, women are regarded as responsible for raising their children, submissive to their husbands or other male family elders, and responsible for various household duties. Therefore, the male members think that given such women's less exposure to social affairs, they are incapable of making logical and beneficial decisions. Unfortunately, this behavior chain has become part of the societal codes, historically contrary to the actual and core cultural codes.

In addition to women withstanding the worst emotional connection, nowadays, many youngsters are also vulnerable to emotional connection, especially when planning their life goals, including their academic and professional goals, as I have already discussed. However, their parents or other guardians may need to be in a position to mentally support them to achieve those goals.

One of the main reasons is the probable discrepancy between the behavior and expectations of the elders and the mindsets of teenagers. The elders may want their youngsters to become someone entirely as those elders want and expect of them. Which is different from how teenagers want themselves to become in the future. This imbalance leads teenagers to mentally suffer. To better explain the topic, I have narrated a real-life story of an obstinate, yet adored boy, Kamran, from my dad's side's far kinsfolk.

The Adored Kamran:

Kamran resided not far from the village I grew up in a far-flung area of the Khyber Pakhtunkhwa province of Pakistan. Although Kamran was younger than his siblings, he was still several years older than me. As his mother frequently used to tell when she came to see us, Kamran was well known among the kinsfolk for his obstinate behavior. The mother of Kamran was a nice, soft-spoken woman and sympathetic, especially for kids. For behaving so tenderly, especially with kids, I had a lot of respect for her. I can recall how eagerly I would expect her visits so that she might give me cash and treats.

However, I was taken aback by Kamran's stubbornness, given his mother's gentle demeanor. It was well known about Kamran that, once he made up his mind to do something, nothing or no one — not even his devoted parents, who loved Kamran to the moon and back — could ever make him change his mind. Because they all adored him so much, no less than a royal, Kamran's family could accept his obstinate behavior at any cost.

While Kamran's intransigence, which resulted from his royal status in the family, allowed him to enjoy the fruits, he experienced the unfavorable effects of this learned behavior later in life. However, he enjoyed everything because he was the most beloved son and child

EMOTIONAL CONNECTION

in his family, which might have been the root of his rebellious behavior during adulthood. This is because he used to be treated like a prince by his parents and everyone else in the family, which made it easy for him to have anything he desired.

As a result, he had developed the habit of always expecting to be told "yes" to his requests. He had developed the habit of believing he naturally earned what he received. He became so adamant that he could not even fathom having his requests denied because he had never had any of them rejected.

On the other side, Kamran's father was the family's leader. In civilizations where the head of a family enjoyed sole power, he could make choices and have everyone do whatever he decided. Therefore, Kamran's father anticipated that when Kamran became older, he would obey him in the same manner that his father had done when Kamran was younger. He would go beyond to fulfill Kamran's demands to show his son how much he cared for him. As I previously indicated, Kamran's father believed that by showing his kid such obedience as a child, the son would regard his parents similarly as an adult.

After some time, Kamran's elementary school computer teacher advised that the students buy their computers to grasp better how a computer functions. Since his parents wanted him to do well in school and not feel like he lacked anything, Kamran was confident he would receive one. He was correct; he received one from his parents, who gave him an XP Windows 2004 PC with a giant monitor.

I still remember the Microsoft logo as a window with four contrasting flowing colors on each side: green on the upright, red on the upper lift side, blue on the lower lift, and yellow on the bottom right side. When I saw that emblem, I would get filled with emotions since I used to get so delighted when I watched him play video games on his computer and gazed at the entrancing icons on the screen. I also recall how thrilled my other friends and I were to see Kamran navigate the little white arrow toward the music icon. We would eagerly await him to play a song, so this was the most thrilling part.

We would also impatiently wait for him to start playing a Bollywood movie while seated in front of his computer, especially an action film. Overall, noticing all of us encircling Kamran like fans encircling their favorite celebrity, he frequently emphasized his supremacy and how fortunate he was to have a computer at such a young age. He would always feel proud of himself for receiving such an elevated protocol level from his parents and other family members. This imperial behavior, however, later altered his whole attitude and perspective.

For instance, he had grown accustomed to this status. He began to see himself as the same superior and deserving person in the future. However, his feeble mind could not comprehend the other aspects of life, such as how everything passes away gradually but inevitably. He would always speak in a way quite different from the rest of us and talk about his plans and self with the same high status since he thought that his status would last for the rest of his life. On the other hand, we were not as unique as he was; therefore, these words were beyond what our minds could imagine.

When Kamran made such boastful claims, we all would lose ourselves in the sea of our imaginations as we imagined him growing up to be a man of impeccable standards. I would feel less appreciated and underestimate myself if I considered how high his standard might be in the future. Due to his love for learning medical sciences, he would frequently even declare that he would someday serve as Afghanistan's health minister. He would say this because we all thought we would see Afghanistan a developed country once the security situation improved.

However, the obstinate Kamran could only picture himself in the future as the health minister of Afghanistan and was unaware that the wheel of life was turning quickly with zero angles and could shift his destiny at any time. He was unaware that his time as a prince would only last a short while. Even so, Kamran stopped living like a prince after elementary and middle school. He began high school by graduating from grade 8 and starting grade 9.

Kamran was enthusiastic about his impending success in grade 9. which was none other than choosing to major in medical sciences as the British educational system has considerably influenced Pakistan's educational system. In this scenario, a student chooses their area of study in grade 9 and continues to study in grades 11 and 12 of college and an undergraduate degree. In contrast, schools in the United States of America consider grades 11 and 12 as high school. While moving on to grade 9 seemed exciting to Kamran, it marked a significant turning point in his life as he had to deal independently with previously unheard-of real-world situations. For instance, Kamran saw a sudden rise in his parents' expectations of him and a minor change in how they treated him as their grown son and a high school student.

After realizing an emotionally connected behavioral gap between him and his parents due to the mismatch between Kamran's acquired behavior and his parents' expectations of him, Kamran had a critical turning point in his life. He realized he was no longer a child and had reached adulthood. Because of this, he would frequently unexpectedly quarrel with his parents about every small thing they could not reasonably expect of him as their grown son. Then, his parents considered his impolite behavior to be unethical.

Like, Kamran berated his parents for not having a good education. He frequently got into pointless arguments with his parents about how they ought to act, behave, and raise their children, etc. However, Kamran's parents were not prepared for their beloved son to behave so acrimoniously as an adult. They believed that he would be just as collected and composed as they had anticipated when he grew up. His parents only wanted to see him happy, so they gave him everything.

They, therefore, assumed that their son would develop into an obedient individual with proper manners. But destiny had other plans and steered events in the son's and his parents' entirely different directions. At this point, Kamran saw a gradual decline in his father's and mother's perceptions of his princely status. It was for this reason that Kamran's father, at last, understood the necessity of changing his son's ingrained behavior. To conform to his expectations, Kamran's father wanted to alter Kamran's behavior. Although Kamran was an adult at the time and his mind was no longer susceptible to change, it was tough for Kamran's father to change his son's behavior. The fact that Kamran's father had no other choice made it imperative for him to do it.

After some time, Kamran's father and mom understood that they would use every method to improve their son's unpleasant behavior. After repeated unsuccessful attempts to change their son's rude behavior, influenced by his obstinacy, they finally gave up. The endeavor to correct their son eventually became burdensome for Kamran's father. They then realized that they, as parents, had failed to instill in their kids the fundamental morals and obligations of parents. They were not psychologically prepared to treat Kamran with the same dominance he had experienced as a child.

On the other hand, Kamran's mental health had been severely impacted because he could no longer revel in his superiority, especially compared to the other children in his family. So much so that his father's rapid change in behavior left him feeling mentally harmed. Being the most beloved child in his family, Kamran could never have predicted the unheard-of shift in his father's behavior. Personally, having closely followed this entire story, if I had to assign responsibility for Kamran's actions and his experiences, I would hold his parents and elders responsible. Kamran would not have adopted such harsh behavior if his parents and elders had not raised him with such skewed and excessive superiority that he had failed to recognize himself and prepare for the worst in his maturity.

Such a behavior was triggered by his royal status as a young child. This is because, during his childhood, Kamran was emotionally and physically dependent on his parents. He could not carry even a tiny and shared responsibility on his own. Even later, he was financially dependent on his parents despite being mature. He was incapable of independently making decisions for his life due to his emotional attachment and reliance on his parents; he had no idea about making logical decisions or when to do what.

Therefore, when Kamran was a child, his parents misjudged their son's behavior as an adult, which was the complete reverse of what they had anticipated. However, this phenomenon created a negative psychological imbalance between Kamran's learned habits and his parents' expectations. As they were to him as a kid and teenager, their parents wanted him to follow their rules with such honesty. However, by that point, it was too late, as he had already reached adulthood and had acquired a personality that was nearly difficult for Kamran's parents to alter.

For instance, Kamran's mother once complained about Kamran's behavior when she came to our home. She added that nobody was at home the day before when they were expecting their family friends, not even Kamran's parents, who had been invited to a wedding somewhere else. Kamran had decided to stay home since he thought he would enjoy spending time on his computer.

While Kamran's parents had asked him to welcome the visitors and be with them until they returned before they left, Kamran disregarded his parents' request and kept playing with his computer. Kamran might have felt that his parents would not mind if he ignored the guests, so he disregarded their request. Because Kamran believed the guests could wait until his parents got home. When his parents got home, they were angry at Kamran for not obeying their order and for not staying with the guests. Kamran's careless actions were even noted by the guests.

At that time, Kamran had reached a climax, even though his parents had repeatedly tried to influence him. At precisely this point, Kamran witnessed a crux in his life as he prepared to begin his university studies after graduating high school. As I said earlier, Kamran was already dependent on his parents. Therefore, he expected them to support him in every action he took while choosing his academic path and pursuing his aspirations. He was eager to decide to pursue his goals independently, though. Kamran was perplexed by this predicament and left wondering what to do and what not to do next. The conflict arose from Kamran's desire to become a doctor versus his parents' wish for him to become an engineer.

That is why he majored in medical sciences after he began the ninth grade. After a few days, Kamran's parents decided to meet with their son to go over the course they had picked for him to study when they learned he was about to enroll in an undergraduate program. Thus, the beginning of a new chapter in Kamran's life thrilled both Kamran and his parents. Each of them, especially Kamran's father, was eager to meet and decide Kamran's academic destiny.

This moment drastically altered Kamran's life in a way no one could have predicted. One day, to find Kamran and inform him to meet his father, Kamran's father first requested his wife to see him in his room and then asked his older son Imran to do the same. Kamran was outside in the fields with his friends. After a short while of searching, Imran spotted Kamran in the fields and hurried over to ask to meet his father in his room.

Kamran was so delighted to hear this information that he immediately told his friends he was about to decide on the first step toward his goals. He also boasted that he had correctly imagined himself as Afghanistan's future health minister. Then Kamran hurried home and went straight to his parent's bedroom. Kamran sprinted to greet his father; he was out of breath when he reached the room. Half-dark and already engaged in conversation, Kamran's parents' talk was underway when he entered the room. Kamran interjected, thrilled with the choice regarding his fate. And the conversation continued in the following manner:

Kamran: - "Assalam-o-Alaikum."

Father: - "Wa-Alaikum-Assalaam, common sit."

After replying to his son's Salam, Kamran's father directly went on to declare his vague decision and said…

Father: - "I have decided on a course for you and would like you to get admission to that course"

The choice of Kamran's father seemed ambiguous because he had not yet decided precisely what he wanted Kamran to study.

Abruptly turned pale, then red, and with a shivering voice, Kamran replied.

Kamran: - "Okay."

The hazy decision made by his father shocked Kamran and left him feeling upset. Kamran was confused by his father's choice, and as he was staring down, many thoughts began to float in his head.

Kamran, however, was unaware that his father was clueless about his decision to choose medical sciences as his major in grade 9. Considering how much his father loved him, he was confident that his father would never object to his choice. Kamran had no idea this was a choice that needed to be made with his father's approval. But since he was the family patriarch, Kamran never considered that this act would emotionally harm his father because, as a head of the family, Kamran's father never wanted anyone else to make decisions without consulting him.

Noticing that something must be going on in her son's mind, Kamran's mom suddenly asked her husband on her son's behalf. Thus, she went on to say…

Mom: - "Tell your son exactly which course you want him to study." After hearing this Kamran felt calm because of being tense and he was unable to ask his dad directly about his exact decision.

Father: - "Well, I want my son to study engineering. Because my cousin, who is poorer than us, enrolled his son in engineering. So, I also want to see my son as an engineer in the future and get ahead of my poor cousin's son. Otherwise, he will denigrate us in front of the villagers. Thus, the villagers will mock us for my inability to enroll my son in an engineering course."

Kamran felt as though a hurricane packed with lightning and torrential rain had broken out inside his heart upon hearing his father's clear-cut choice, while he was entirely out of mind — beached like an astronaut hovering in zero gravity in space. Unwillingly nodding his head and muttering…

Kamran: - "Okay."

Kamran, who was upset by his father's choice, reluctantly confirmed the choice…

Mom: - "What makes you put your ego before your son's happiness and aspirations?"

She questioned her husband as she stared at her son's pallid face and understood that her son disliked her husband's decision. And that her husband completely went against what her son desired. Thus, she added...

Mom: - "You are aware that your egoistic rivalry will only benefit your cousin and appease the villagers who care the least about your social image and your son's well-being."

Father: - "Who is the head of the family?"

Counter berated his wife and questioned in a stern voice...

Father: - "You always interfere, but you forget about the breadwinner of this family. I'm Kamran's father — not you, not the villagers. I decide what's right for him, not someone who gets swayed by emotions. He is my son, and as a father, I have the final say. You may not like it, but that is how it is. Kamran cannot make decisions on his own or go against my wishes. Culturally and religiously, I have the supreme authority to decide what is right or wrong for him. After all, I am the one who raised him, loved him, and gave him everything he ever wanted."

He further continued...

Father: - "Kamran should not, as a child, insult his father by making decisions on his own without consulting me, as I do not like it."

When Kamran heard his father's statement, he thought as if he was listening to the speech of a dictator more so than his father, as he later exposed to his mother. Kamran was terrified and upset by his parents' dictatorial statements, and he did not want to watch them continue their disagreement in front of him since it made him feel uneasy. He therefore intervened...

Kamran was so terrified by his father's stern remarks and his mother's innocence that he said...

Kamran: - "I am okay, I am okay."

Kamran affirmed twice. Because he only wished to locate a serene setting. Therefore, Kamran declared...

Kamran: - "I don't care what decision you guys make since you are my elders and I think if I am disrespecting my elders now, others younger than me would be disrespecting me when I turn your age. Moreover, as a son, I'm not expected to speak in my father's presence, regardless of my perspective or understanding of the situation."

Kamran was emotionally imprisoned at this point; caught in a circumstance he had never anticipated. One explanation for this was that his father's serious demeanor had prevented him from considering anything other than keeping his own father's decision. His mother was on the opposite side, but she had little knowledge of general higher education or university programs as she had not attended school at all. Kamran's sentiments for his mother were damaged by her innocence and the fact that his father had been influenced by the rivalry with his cousin. Kamran's objectives were another factor that continuously attracted him. In the meantime, as Kamran was suffocating in his thoughts, his father persuaded Kamran to do as he wanted. Because Kamran's father wanted his wife and son to know that he shared his concern for Kamran's aspirations: and asked…

Father: - "Okay Kamran, tell me which course you are interested in pursuing."

Surprised by the quantum jump in the change of his dad's voice from being harsh behavior toward friendly, he replied…

Kamran: - "I am interested in medical sciences." With this, glory shone on Kamran's face like the sun shining right after the morning dawn.

Even though he heard his son's decision with open ears, yet immediately disagreed and spoke…

Father: - "Kamran, you are right, however, I cannot lose to my poor cousin. Because I truly do not understand how I will deal with the stigma from the villagers if you refuse to study engineering — one of my greatest desires — and end up looking like a failure in comparison to your less fortunate cousin."

Turned her face towards her husband, and then Kamran's mom abruptly interfered:

Mom: - "I am confused and do not understand whether your competition inspired by your egoistic intentions is important or our son's goals and happiness."

Enraged by his wife's words...

Father: - "I know what to do and I will do what I decide, and my son will do what I decide for him. I am the father, and he is the son. My words and decisions are final and unchangeable. And that is the end of the discussion." He slammed the door and walked out of the room.

Now only left the mom and her son in the dimmed room. After a few moments of silence, the mom looked at her son who was looking down while lost in thoughts – thinking about his unknown fate. Kamran's mom said with deep sorrow and a whispering voice:

Mom: - "I know what is going on in your mind right now and I completely realize that you are hurt by your dad's decision and his harsh words. But let me tell you one thing, neither I can do anything for you nor you. Because you are a teenager, and I am a woman. You know that is our only fault." Referring to her husband, she added, "These men think they are always right, and they are the only decision-makers. But I assure you everything will be all right and you will do your best and make us proud."

After a while of silence and a deep sigh, Kamran said...

Kamran: - "I can do my best only if I go with my decision and pursue my goals. And I am sure if I do that, Dad will be disappointed with me because he will lose his competition with his cousin. But if I go with Dad's decision, I will never be able to do as best as I would do with my personal decision. In that case, I will end up suffering for the rest of my life. I believe I will do my best if my dad lets me pursue my goals and decide on my own because I live for myself and you all. I do not care about what others say about us. For me, our happiness and success are more important than society. Now, Mom, you tell me what I should do? Sacrifice my dreams to please society or shall I pursue my goals?"

With this, Kamran hugged his mom and burst into tears while putting his head on his mom's shoulder. At this moment, his dad had heard everything and suddenly entered the room and exclaimed!

Father: - "What are you mom and son planning to decide? are you going to defy my rules? Are you going to break the rules laid by our ancestors, which is to obey the decision of the head of the family? If so then all right, do whatever you want but make sure you leave my house because in this house only my decision should be followed." The father banged the door again and left the room."

After hearing what her husband said, she suddenly burst into tears and told Kamran…

Mom: - "Son, do whatever your dad wants you to do. We have no other option except to adhere to your dad's decision."

Kamran: - "Okay." and then he quietly left the room after accepting his mom's request without showing any reaction.

It was the transitional period between nighttime and afternoon when dusk was splattered with dull light. Kamran stepped outdoors, went to the closest wheat fields, and sat there awhile. When frustrated, Kamran frequently spent time alone in the fields to clear his head. He was peacefully accompanied by the fall-gloomy season's clouds, which covered the blue sky with their dark and grey hues while he sat on the fields. Kamran was alone in the fields, acting like a lost orphan in an uncharted city with no past or destiny.

He was suddenly pelted with water from the drizzling rain as he continued to sit, unaware that it was happening to him. The fact that he was completely drenched from head to toe only became apparent later. At that time, he was still a family prince but was now viewed as a rebel, and as time went on, people began to see him as an anti-cultural individual. The mental strain Kamran was experiencing had already driven him insane. He had no capacity for clear thought.

While sitting in the fields under the drizzle, one of Kamran's friends, Karim, saw him and suddenly rushed towards him.

Karim: - "Hey, have you lost your mind or what? Why are you sitting here at this time in the rain? You are splashed with water. Go home now and change your clothes."

Kamran was merely staring at Karim, and he was not able to respond. At this, Karim got scared and shook him with the trembling movement of his hands and said,

THE DEATH WITHIN

Karim: - "Hey, are you okay?"

Kamran only replied to this…

Kamran: - "Yes, leave me alone."

To inform Kamran's mother that her son was sitting in the fields by himself and was completely drenched in water, Karim left him alone and sprinted toward his mother. Kamran's mother was startled by hearing this bad news and fled to see her son immediately after hearing the news. Other women in the house screamed and commanded her to cover her face because she was leaving the house at this precise moment without having her hair and face covered.

But Karim, an outspoken boy, exclaimed that these people were more concerned about the uncovered hair of Kamran's mom than what both Kamran and his mom were going through. However, she was unconcerned and sprinted to her son, cradling him in her arms like a newborn after seeing her mother for the first time. She began sobbing, holding her son, who was crying with her, and placing his head on her lap.

Following her announcement to the family members, Kamran's mom developed a fever the following morning, which also spread to Kamran. The family members tried questioning Kamran about his condition, but he could not speak clearly. They all stood there in disbelief. Nevertheless, his mother remained truthful when she explained, "My kid cannot speak since he endured constant pressure and his voice was being muffled and not heard, which culminated in his silence." She was mistaken, though, because nobody discovered the truth before the boy's admission to a hospital.

When the doctor took his x-ray, it was discovered that he had neck thyroid issues that needed removal. The prospect that the little boy could get cancer due to his thyroid condition made this news incredibly frightening and alarming for Kamran's family. Kamran was unaware of this, though. He endured mental anguish for the rest of his life. He was no longer the prince of his family or the chatty young man who had boasted of his promising future and lofty standards. Both his father and Kamran were unsuccessful in competing egotistically against their less fortunate cousins. Instead, he experienced an extended period of acute despair and felt like a failure because his career was over. That despair destroyed Kamran's overall peace of mind.

After watching the entire ordeal, Kamran's family realized that Kamran's father had been a utilitarian and egoistic rather than a loving father. Even Kamran's father had realized that his son and wife's happiness was of no importance to him; only his ego and the approval of society did. Since childhood, Kamran has been emotionally connected to his royal status in his family. This also affected his siblings about their parents' biased attitude towards them made Kamran superior to them in the eyes of their parents and other family members.

However, suppose Kamran's parents – especially his father did not give their son a princely status with opposite expectations. In that case, Kamran migh not have taken his family members' soft behavior towards him for granted and thus suffered in adulthood. It was unfortunate that nothing could be changed at that time. While his son eventually developed mental illness, Kamran's father developed worse conditions while battling his ego, which always blamed him.

Lessons Learned:

- How adults treat children when they are young influences how they learn to behave. Because kids learn more from seeing their elders' personalities and deeds than they do from listening to what they have to say.
- Teens' mental agony is frequently caused by their emotional attachment to their elders, who frequently take advantage of them for their desires while sacrificing the teenagers' dreams.
- When teenagers are emotionally constrained, success becomes more challenging for them.
- The people whose behavior causes us the greatest of mental suffering are those with whom we have close emotional connections or those who have us more closely.

- Stubbornness can sometimes be advantageous when motivated by the desire to accomplish the intended goals.
- Frequently, conflicts arise between parents and a particular child because of parents' little affection for one child while disregarding others. The remaining marginalized children grow up in such a way that they simply follow the usual life routine. These sidelined children are more likely to obey such conventional routine than the adored children.
- In conclusion, parents should comprehend that genuine success and pleasure are anchored in doing what is in their family's best interests and what makes them happy. Not acting in ways that impress society while it is unconcerned, impressing society even at the expense of one's own or their loved one's mental well-being, is a complete failure. It is OK to love and care for children as they grow up. However, it is unfair to favor one child over others while showing partial affection to one and expect that child to change to suit his or her parents' preferences. A better approach is to treat all children equally and nurture them so that they can simultaneously feel loved and respected, as well as learn how to balance their needs with those of their parents.

Self-Esteem

TEENAGERS, ESPECIALLY THOSE between twelve and seventeen, have elevated self-respect and self-esteem. If we observe them closely, we will notice them consistently behaving as if they act as the lead hero in a movie. As an illustration, from doing their hair to strolling down the street, being treated, and engaging with others. Most of the time, they even tend to act, dress, and behave like their role models – their favorite movie stars.

When a child is alone, we may more easily witness this behavior. Most of the time, they will talk or sing to themselves. Girls will frequently dance to the beat of the songs they murmur. Such children are, however, often viewed as abnormal or mentally ill by many people. As these kids sing or talk to themselves, people may assume something is wrong with them. Nonetheless, the fact is that those kids enjoy their own company in that small world they create for themselves.

Those teens constantly attempt to make themselves appear attractive and pursue activities that make them happy. This is a unique technique for defining a person's personality and way of living. As a result, those types of teenagers develop a sense of self-respect, encouraging them to develop self-esteem and confidence.

Therefore, they develop a distinct perception of themselves in the eyes of their family and peers. Even in class, their classmates in schools or colleges have a unique perception of who they are. However, these teenagers frequently become frustrated when their well-built public images suffer harm.

This is due to their solid mental connections to the perceptions of their typical personalities. Because of this, they assume that their real personality is what they think it is or what other people think it is. But we humans are neither what we assume we are nor what others believe we are; instead, we are what we think other people think we are. We are psychologically held captive by other people's views and judgments of us, which is why this is the case.

Since the perceptions and opinions of others about our personalities control and mold our actions and ideas. Therefore, teenagers' mental freedom and self-esteem should be valued by their parents and other elderly family members. Suppose teenagers have a sense of self-esteem and freedom. In that case, they will be independent of the mental slavery brought on by the opinions of others.

People's Opinions:

The opinions and expectations of teenagers may also result in their mental enslavement. What older people think of teens and what they do with them differ significantly. This conundrum is brought on by the fact that most older people expect their teens to abstain from smoking. Still, the elders themselves may either smoke now, or they might have smoked in the past. The elders' expectations of the teens' behavior and mentality differ from what they believe is true. The teens might think critically and argue that those elders themselves smoked, so teens should also smoke. It is also possible that they will believe that because the elderly smoke, they do not have the authority to forbid teenagers from doing the same.

Another situation where expectations and perspective clash are when family members expect their children to prosper and do well, for example, in academics, but they have a pessimistic impression of teenagers. This indicates that although elders have high expectations for their teenagers' success in academics and other domains, they have less trust in their teenagers due to their pessimistic perceptions about those teens. Because of this, teenagers' self-esteem and confidence are indirectly but severely devastated. Furthermore, teenagers harbor a long-lasting resentment of their elders that they create and retain in their minds.

When teenagers' actions and thoughts are more reliant on the opinions of others, particularly their elders, it adds to their lack of confidence in them. These teenagers frequently lose their sense of self-worth and their capacity for autonomous thinking ability and self-assured behavior, which, among others, is a significant reason for their lack of self-esteem. Teenagers lose their self-confidence, which causes them to feel dread and trepidation before taking action. Thus, young people's attitudes are developed in a manner that does not prepare them to embrace the unheard-of. When teenagers act or make decisions independently in the family, they frequently experience fear of elders and parents. They think that if they act without their parent's permission, their parents will get offended, which is why teenagers fear.

Teenagers frequently make an effort to cut emotional chords with their parents. Because they feel psychologically constrained and uncomfortable when their parents are around. Similar to how children's dread of police law enforcement causes them to have a fearful perception of the police. Like poor self-esteem and confidence affect teenagers, these teens also experience negative influences from their parents. This is why teens also cannot share their inner feelings with their elders due to their fear of disrespecting their parents. This is the primary reason such teens choose to be alone and thus become introverted.

Teenagers' discomfort with their parents' behavior is also because, despite not always being capable of cognitively complying with their demands, teenagers sometimes do so out of respect for their parents. In fact, teenagers are compelled by social norms that demand reverence for elders, even though those teenagers may do so reluctantly. Because of such behavior, even when parents are at fault, teenagers are expected to respect them. I refer to "paid respect" when parents compliment their teenagers for acting delicately and respectfully without knowing that it was imposed upon them.

Paid respect is when teenagers are psychologically coerced into deferring to their elders out of a desire to uphold social norms or appease elders. By engaging in this behavior, teenagers are only serving their elders' egos by making themselves mentally unhappy. Mainly if a teenager is more concerned with their self-esteem. However, due to a certain sense of self-respect and logic, this is not a teenager's arrogance. Children should avoid engaging in this behavior because they often develop the same personality traits into maturity. Since they become depressed and give in to demands made of them without rational argument.

Comparison:

The incapacity of teens to argue prudently might be attributed to the fact that parents frequently compare their children to other children. This comparison might be made regarding their academic performance, sports performance, usual behavior, or other intelligence. Some youngsters are motivated when the comparison is regarded as beneficial to them.

When a top-performing student is compared with a low-performing student, the top performer feels more content and motivated. On the contrary, comparing a weak and low-performing child to a more polite, clever, or great athletic child might be detrimental to his mental health and self-esteem. The low-performing child could suffer from an inferiority complex. Also, his self-esteem plummets as he feels less deserving when compared to the children that exceed him.

That kid must be better at something else. Yet, his parents continuously compare him with other kids based on a particular skill he lacks and could improve. The fact that parents desire their children to achieve well and be better at one thing is mainly motivated by the parents' egoistic behavior. Therefore, parents should strive to identify their children's one particular skill they are good at and encourage them to focus on using their potential and abilities to accomplish what they enjoy and are adept at.

Every child is unique and should be treated based on their unique traits. My advice for elderly people is to be the person they wished for themselves when they were kids. Because when we were children, we sought elderly people to be gentle and righteous and be the ones whom we could feel mentally peaceful with. Therefore, if an elder is harsh with children, he must remember his childhood. During childhood, kids are more satisfied and happier when their elders sympathize with them based on their childhood experiences.

But unfortunately, most parents not only compare their children to those of other people, but they also compare their children to one another. Such parents' behavior could foster rivalry and competition among siblings as they will tend to surpass each other in every aspect. This behavior may reduce the level of confidence in kids.

Lack of Trust:

When a youngster lacks confidence, he develops skepticism of his elders. The untrustworthy behavior of elders toward their children remains the root of the problem. As previously stated, such an unwelcome behavior might take the shape of discriminatory treatment of children or comparing them to other children. As a result, children lose trust in their elders since they no longer feel emotionally peaceful and safe with them. Because such children's inner voices get silenced, and their sentiments repressed. Not only is children's trust eroded, but so is their emotional reliance on their elders.

When a child's emotional bond with his elders deteriorates, the child loses self-esteem. This is because the emotional bond between a kid and his elders is firmly bound by the knot of trust. Once that knot is broken, the emotional connection between a child and elders no longer exists. Thus, it is evident that for elders to emotionally connect with their children, they must make them feel loved and cherished. They should also pay close attention to ensuring that their children's self-esteem is appropriately cared for. Otherwise, when it comes to damaging a child's self-esteem, the effects may be equally detrimental to both the child and the elders.

Such effects for parents include a communication rift between them and their children. Furthermore, parents may lose their authority status in their children's eyes. The children may no longer trust their parents' advice for improvement. Children with low self-esteem, on the other hand, are more likely to engage in inappropriate behaviors such as lying, stealing, and cursing others. Because they have become accustomed to having their self-esteem lowered.

As a result, they look to denigrate others to demonstrate their superiority. Such a behavior satisfies them because they know they will achieve their retribution and find inner peace. This is due to their propensity to continuously think poorly about themselves and others. Another cause for such children's poor self-esteem might be that parents and other family elders try to cover their flaws by blaming children. While the children usually fail to appropriately convey the problem and demonstrate that they are not the actual perpetrators, they merely experience inner agony.

As a result, it is completely unreasonable for elders to try to prove their children wrong or to blame them for their own mistakes. This might tarnish children's images and undermine their self-esteem, destroying their inner peace and happiness. The underlying agony of children is exacerbated when their elders first blame or put them in difficulty, then act softly to appear to favor the children. The reason for this is that the elderly gain satisfaction through the disguised behavior of acting tenderly with their children, which is damaging to the mental peace of the children in the long run. When the mental health of children is not peaceful, they tend to develop several other shortcomings, for example, losing analytical and decision-making skills.

Analytical Skills:

Throughout my life in Afghanistan, I have been surrounded by people whose ideas are entwined with emotions and cultural rules. I have concluded that children in those societies are nurtured strongly, emphasizing societal values, emotions, and cultural behavior and codes. However, it is difficult for children who have an inherent trait of being mentally free to be content with their surroundings in those societies.

According to my observations, such children are eager to live in the West because they believe they can gain mental freedom and live a life devoid of any societal code of behavior. This is because, in the West, most decisions and perspectives are formed and developed based on one's subjective viewpoint rather than sentiments.

As a result, the West is technologically more advanced than most parts of the East. Because unlike specific individuals in underdeveloped nations such as Afghanistan, who make decisions based on past events, people in the West make decisions based on what is going to happen in the future. This may be true because some Afghans believe that the codes left in perpetuity should be treasured and obeyed and that no one has the authority to go against them by any chance.

Because regardless of how rational they are, debates over those codes are often regarded as inappropriate behavior. This sort of behavior results in the erosion of youngsters' analytical skills. They are given directions from an early age to keep their analytical talents inactive, so their thinking capacity is constrained to mainstream norms. Not only that, but a lack of analytical skills may impair other abilities, such as teens' decision-making abilities.

Decision-Making Skills:

I have observed families who adhere to a specific set of norms due to my close observations of village life in Afghanistan. As stated in previous sections, the authority to decide lies entirely with the head of the family, with consultation with other older family members. Teenagers in such families are rarely allowed to speak up and share their thoughts on crucial issues.

This is because teens are considered weak and immature when providing appropriate suggestions. And this is true because kids' self-esteem is shattered at first, which leads to damage to their analytical abilities and broader thinking capacity, followed by the inability to form beneficial assessments and make sound decisions.

On the one hand, family members wreck children's self-esteem and thinking abilities owing to society's standards. They then regard them as incompetent and immature, causing teens to lose faith in their elders and parents and thus end up suffering within. The ramifications of this phenomenon for teens linger longer than predicted, and those youngsters still have the same dread of expressing their thoughts and speaking out in adulthood.

Not just for family concerns, but if a choice concerning a teenager's personal life is made, he may be denied the right to stand out for himself and express his thoughts about his life. Because the elders believe that, given the teen's fragile thinking, whatever the elders decide is for the teenager's advantage and that the teenager is incapable of understanding the significance of the family members' decisions.

Nonetheless, such a family member's attitude undermines a teenager's decision-making skills and damages his confidence in himself. As a result, he builds a negative and terrible self-perception and constantly doubts his interpersonal abilities. Even when a teenager reaches maturity, he may be unable to examine and understand each situation that comes his way. His thinking abilities will become limited merely to his family rules, and he may be unable to think freely and independently. However, if the teenager is mature enough to manage the circumstances in his childhood and ensure that his self-esteem is not harmed by his family members' actions. He may still suffer due to the status quo followed by his family members.

Ways to Overcome?

While teens' self-esteem is affected by inappropriate behaviors from their elders and parents, there are viable solutions. Based on what I have discovered, communication is vital between a teenager and his or her elders or parents in a household. This is because many misunderstandings and disagreements emerge due to inadequate communication between elders or parents and their children. Therefore, the following points need to be considered by elders or parents when dealing with their kids.

- **Parents Should Deal with Their Anger:** We agree to care for the energy of anger as it occurs and acknowledge and transform the seeds of anger that lie deep in our consciousness since we are aware that anger prevents communication and causes pain. When rage arises, we choose not to do or say anything but to practice mindful breathing or mindful walking and accept, embrace, and gaze deeply into our anger. We shall learn to see people we believe are the source of our rage with compassion. Additionally, I advise parents that their communication and behavior with their children should not come at the expense of their children's mental peace and happiness.

- **Parents Should Maintain a Proper Communication Channel:** Recognizing that a lack of communication usually results in separation and misery, we are devoted to practicing compassionate listening and loving speaking. We will learn to listen thoroughly without judging or responding and refrain from saying things that may cause division or tear down communication between parents and their children. We shall make every effort to maintain open lines of communication and to reconcile and resolve all disagreements, no matter how little they are.
- **Teenagers Should be Valued:** One of the mainstream inappropriate behaviors of elders is that they mainly exploit the politeness of their teens. Such exploitation leads to damage to the self-esteem and self-respect of teenagers. Once teenagers feel that their worth diminishes, they lose their trust and emotional bond with their parents and elders. Therefore, maintaining the self-esteem of teenagers is vital both for parents and elders.

Parental Role

THE BEHAVIOR OF parents with one another shapes the course of their children's mindsets and personalities. Such behavior can either be positive or negative. How husband and wife treat one another in front of their child directly influences the child's mindset about his parents' behavior and outlook on life. These changes could last for a lifetime. Therefore, parents need to behave appropriately in front of their children so that the children build a positive impression of their parents. Even if the parents are having troubles and quarrels with one another. In front of their kids, they must keep that grudge or disagreement aside and behave as if everything is going well and nothing wrong has happened.

This is possible only when both parents have a solid mutual understanding and high maturity levels to empathize with one another. For this reason, we must find the right partner for ourselves. The right to find the right partner lies solely with both girls and boys. It is exclusively a teenager's choice to find the right life partner for themself. Nonetheless, in many parts of Afghanistan, people still follow the codes under which parents and family elders are the only ones who own the authority to decide on a girl or boy's partner.

However, in rare cases, the boy is asked about the girl his family wants him to marry and whether he likes her. But in the girl's case, the family rarely asks her if she likes the boy whose family proposes to her family to marry their daughter. In this case, it is possible that the girl likes another boy, or the boy likes another girl. But based on their intentions to show society how adherent they are to the societal codes; the girl must accept to marry the boy that the family elders and her parents have chosen for her.

But why would others decide on whom we should marry and live for a lifetime with? The answer is simple; for most families, fulfilling egoistic desires by impressing society is a top priority and more important than the satisfaction and happiness of their kids.

This is why many youths are vulnerable to societal norms and are unhappy after their marriage. For example, a boy may love one girl, but his parents and family elders would have decided to marry him to another girl he may not like. Later in life, that boy may disagree with his wife on every minor issue as they may have been forcefully married. This is a typical case in the context of those teens who, later in life, are exposed to a different environment. In the new environment, they meet more advanced people with sophisticated lifestyles.

For instance, a boy from a village marries a girl from the same neighborhood with the same mentality, behavior, and lifestyle. In case, after marriage, that boy gets higher education, visits unfamiliar places, and meets new and advanced people. Exposure to a different environment with people of advanced lifestyles may change his personality, affecting his relationship with his wife. Suppose the boy gets a professional office job and sees a female coworker with a fine sense of humor, soft behavior, and ambitious standards; he may start comparing her with his wife. As a result, he may be negatively perceiving his wife as uneducated or less modernized compared to the other girl he meets in his workplace.

However, I do not blame either the boy or the girl, but rather their parents. I regard such parental decisions as entirely being influenced by their ego. I have noticed that parents aim to put themselves ahead of others in the societal race. This is useless for them and only victimizes young people to the social race. This is why I previously stressed the significance of parents' gentle demeanor toward their children.

The parents' actions will first victimize their children. Then the children will follow in their parents' footsteps when they become parents. In turn, the chain of such behavior will become more common and mainstream. Like many other mainstream norms, it may become a significant part of the culture if left unquestioned. Furthermore, I frequently consider the impact of poor parental communication on a child, particularly one influenced by the gap in the perspectives of husband and wife.

Opinion Disparity:

As I previously stated, a young boy and a young girl have the right to pick the perfect spouse. By "right partner," I mean someone who shares a similar or matching level of thinking, comprehension, humor, and maturity. If these four features of a couple are satisfactory, they are less likely to have disagreements in life. Even if they disagree, they will strive to understand one another before resolving the matter. As a result, a person must determine whether or not their prospective life partner possesses those four characteristics.

To achieve this, a boy and a girl must communicate and understand each other's expectations of their relationship before their lifelong commitment to marriage. Otherwise, if a couple does not have equal or matching levels of understanding, maturity, humor, and thinking, they are more likely to disagree on anything in life, which might even destroy their marriage. Ultimately, resolving such situations will be quite challenging for them.

Even if they strive to reconcile their differences, they may try to harmonize their degrees of humor, understanding, thinking, and maturity levels. As a result, either the husband or wife but one of them will have to drop to the level of the other in terms of those four aspects. Otherwise, if a couple does not have similar or matching levels of understanding, maturity, humor, and thinking, they are more likely to disagree on everything in life, which might even destroy their marriage, however.

Eventually, resolving these kinds of issues will be challenging for them. Even if they strive to overcome their differences, they may try to harmonize their degrees of humor, understanding, thinking, and maturity. As a result, as I mentioned, either the husband or wife must come down to the level of the other in terms of those four categories. Otherwise, the consequences may lead to several other issues, such as poor communication.

Improper Communication:
Knowing that poor communication between a husband and wife can cause pain for their children, speaking gently and maturely can be highly beneficial to children's mental health. Children are always delighted when they witness their parents communicating properly and understanding one another. Because we may have noticed as children that we were adversely affected when an acute family issue was discussed in front of us. Take, for example, any financial issue in a household. Also, any dispute or serious debate between our parents or other older family members would severely impact our mental health.

Therefore, family elders and parents must understand when and how to speak, particularly in front of children. However, questions concerning children's opinions might be posed to help them believe that their elders and parents value their opinions. This makes them feel valued and emotionally connected to the family. Nonetheless, adequate understanding among family members, particularly between a husband and wife, is essential – not just for them as a couple but also for their children's mental health and behavior.

Meanwhile, children prefer to accept anything when requested in a warm and kind tone rather than being commanded. Even if they are provided with pleasant things, they are more likely to reject them if the communication is delivered in a stern tone or an authoritative manner. However, if they are provided with something they do not want, but the tone of communication is warm and kind, they will immediately accept it. This is why I emphasized the importance of parents and elders behaving gently in front of their children. Because children learn more by observing than by hearing, as they replicate their elders and imitate behaviors that they observe and engage in their surroundings. Several hazardous ways to communicate exist, including giving advice.

Parental Advice:

By displaying good behavior, elders and parents can avoid constantly advising their children to behave appropriately. While the advice is considered beneficial, in my opinion it is an indirect affront, insult, or mild curse. I am not in favor of elders advising their children, but I agree that elders should behave the way they want their children to behave. In this way, children may see and emulate their elders' positive behavior. Another reason is that when children are advised, they suffer from an inferiority complex and begin to feel they have done something wrong. As a result, children feel guilty even if they have done nothing wrong.

On top of that, elders advise their children to avoid making mistakes. For those children, the desire to avoid making mistakes indicates a lack of willingness to try new things. Avoiding trying new things means missing opportunities to gain experience. Finally, a child cannot develop or grow due to a lack of learning and experience. Instead, he will be mentally imprisoned by family behavior and societal norms for the rest of his life.

Another effect of advising children is that a wider distance between them and their parents could arise. When a child receives continual bits of advice, he often tries to cover up his mistakes rather than genuinely trying to correct himself. The root cause of this behavior is apparent: after receiving repeated advice, kids feel guilty. As a result, they only strive to disguise friendly behavior to receive praise and be seen as polite. However, the majority of parents and elders still hold the belief that children must be advised to avoid developing into rebellious adolescents.

Yet because of their egoistic and utilitarian behavior, parents and elders tend to stress advising children. Because as we can see, parents frequently advise trying to mentally control their children by making them feel they must pay attention to and follow what their parents and elders say. However, a generation gap has caused a significant difference between the mindsets of today's teenagers from their parents and elders. This is the main reason many parents and elders are mentally unprepared to let go of control over their children; parents and elders behave in such a way.

However, there are also additional consequences, such as teenagers' propensity for lying. As an example, suppose a child makes a mistake despite being advised. If his parents learn about his mistake, the child can feel embarrassed. In this situation, he is more likely to lie to cover up his mistake. The child's tendency to lie will gradually grow and become an inevitable component of his life.

The Bottom Line:

A healthy and profound understanding between a husband and wife is essential for their kid's whole life, especially in terms of his mental health. To establish outstanding behaviors in a child, parents must demonstrate good behavior themselves first rather than straightway advising their child. Because a child learns more by observing his surroundings than by listening. As a result, both verbal and non-verbal good communications are the key to an enjoyable life for parents and their children.

Unfortunately, in countries, like Afghanistan, parents believe they are always right in their decisions. However, the world is changing rapidly, and even a little child can distinguish between good and evil. Because the internet and social media dominate modern-day society, children are acutely aware of issues that even their parents from the twentieth century are unaware of. This is why I define the internet as the devil's network, as it provides everything irrespective of how unethical they are.

This is why I suggest parents and family elders handle their children with balance - neither earnestly nor overly affectionately. Understanding authentic religious principles, trustworthy cultural standards, and spiritual practices, and instilling these in children, is the most incredible method to keep a balance. This is beneficial for establishing fundamental principles in children and restoring their natural productivity and creativity. Thus, children's attention will never be diverted by other frivolous and dangerous things, such as the internet and being victimized by elderly people to impress society.

Ultimately being forced to isolate themselves from the world to take refuge in today's dangerous things, such as the internet. Thus, parents and family elders should not believe that they must always be prioritized and respected at the expense of their children's mental health. Children's mental health is far more essential than trivial superstitions beliefs or forced respect for elders.

Females' Vulnerability

EVEN THOUGH IT is widely perceived that women and girls in the far-flung localities of Afghanistan frequently get less exposure for fundamental rights such as education and work etc., which is considered the main reason behind their suffering. Many people consider this issue as something inclined by religious principles or cultural codes. It is, therefore, crucial to first identify the underlying causes of why girls and women are treated differently.

Unfortunately, a common misconception is that females in the majority of these areas are denied access to their fundamental rights because of cultural or religious obligations. To me, this perception is wholly untrue. Given this is a complex topic, let us begin by discussing why and how girls from those backward communities suffer. Does the girls' lack of access to fundamental rights result from cultural codes and religious obligations? Finding answers to these questions is essential to draw attention to.

The significance of this topic is also underscored by the fact that depriving girls of their fundamental rights causes them to be unfairly treated, which leads to their suffering. Therefore, this section's primary purpose is to highlight that girls experience mental suffering due to being unfairly treated through less access to their rights. Although the residents of those communities practice Islam, based on my observation and understanding of the true religious principles and cultural norms, girls and women should have equal rights to social benefits like education and many more.

Therefore, holding a bias against the rights of any human is unfair. Because if we take Islam as an example, the Holy Quran clearly states that both males and females have distinct but relevant rights to social benefits, and thus, both must be equally treated. As the Holy Quran states:

- Whoever does evil then not he will be recompensed but (the) like thereof; and whoever does righteous (deeds), of male or female, while he (is) a believer, then those will enter Paradise, they will be given provision in it without an account. (40:40)

The above verse from the Holy Quran emphasizes that Islam upholds equality and does not differentiate between individuals based on gender or perceived superiority. From this, we can also conclude that males and females have similar rights to social benefits, including access to education, participation in decision-making, fair treatment, and other privileges. I use "similar" instead of "equal" to women's rights here. Given their biological structures, males can perform tasks that women cannot. However, due to how their biological structures work, there are certain activities that only women can perform.

This reality is frequently illustrated by traits like emotional fortitude, physical toughness, or the unique characteristics of birthing in women. It is a prevalent belief that women are emotionally stronger than males overall, which makes them more tolerant and resilient. However, men, too, can perform specific physical tasks more effectively than women because of their more significant physical potential. Therefore, men and women should be given their fundamental social rights, applicable and analogous rights, per their unique emotional, physical, and biological structures.

Nonetheless, in many places of today's Taliban-ruled Afghanistan, some individuals pacify the Taliban's restrictive polices concerning women, such as the ban on girls' education. There is still a social belief that women should not work in offices or locations where they stay alongside Naa-mahram (a person with whom it is lawful for a muslim woman to marry) and should thus remain in households shrouded in veils. Many people believe that because women are meant to stay home, they should not work or study and only take care of household responsibilities.

They forget, however, that wearing a veil or practicing modesty is not only for women but also for males. If women are supposed to cover their bodies - which is ethically and rationally beneficial for their protection from evil eye or to avoid arousing men's sexual temptation. Men should be modest as well by taking care of their eyes and minds. When men see a lady without a cover or wearing enticing clothing, they must keep their gaze down. In this regard, Allah SWT commands in the Holy Quran:

- O children of Adam, we have provided you with garments to cover your bodies, as well as for luxury. But the best garment is the garment of righteousness. These are some of God's signs, that they may take heed. (7:26)

Quranic verses, in many cases, touch only briefly on profound subjects, necessitating thorough and knowledgeable interpretation for proper understanding. Sometimes, the Quranic verses are interpreted differently highlighting various interpretations and meanings. However, my understanding suggests that in the preceding verse, Allah commands all humans by calling them the children of Adam. The term "children of Adam" refers to both males and women. This clearly demonstrates that both men and women should be treated equally and provided with their relevant rights. Thus, both need to follow modesty.

- O humanity! Indeed, we created you from a male and a female and made you into peoples and tribes so that you may get to know one another. Surely the noblest of you in the sight of Allah is the most righteous among you. Allah is truly All-Knowing, All-Aware. (49:13)

Allah SWT clearly refers to males and females in the preceding verse from the Holy Quran, rather than just males or females. This demonstrates how Islam regards men and women, with neither being superior. Furthermore, it is evident from the preceding verse that Islam favors righteousness over social status or age range. However, elites and certain religious masters claim to live according to Islamic principles, their perspective surprisingly is antithetical to Quranic teachings and more of man-made social beliefs.

While the required modesty applies to both men and women, the verse underlines that the best clothing of modesty and holiness is the garment of righteousness. In this context, righteousness denotes the value of humility and purity of mind and spirit rather than only outward appearance. While outer appearance can often be deceiving, only Allah knows about the purity of heart and soul.

Therefore, whenever a significant issue is mentioned in a specific verse of the Holy Quran, it must be understood and inferred with the assistance of scholars. This is because most of the verses in the Holy Quran were revealed to address a specific tribe or nation's concern. There is a possibility that the problem does not exist now and that the verse only pertained to that historical period and those unique individuals, their culture, lifestyle, and so on. However, regarding the ethical relevance of such verses, they are applicable even to contemporary life, for example, how to behave with our elders, children, neighbors, etc.

When discussing the sufferings of women due to misinterpretation of some religious concepts or cultural norms in Afghan society, it is crucial to remember that Islam values education for both men and women. Women who suffer from this issue are subjected to agony and mental brutality. Furthermore, denying education to their daughters, if by any Muslims, demonstrates their disdain and disobedience to the basic Quranic principles. In the Holy Quran, for example, Allah clearly distinguishes between educated and uneducated human beings regardless of their gender.

- Say: 'Can those who have the knowledge and those who do not be alike?' So only the wise do receive the admonition. (39:9)

In many parts of Afghanistan, girls are only permitted to study until middle or high school in many villages, nevertheless. The notion is that once they reach maturity, their parents rarely let them pursue further schooling. This is mainly because of their marriage. At a young age in maturity, parents want their daughters to be married. This may be the case since getting married in one's early twenties is viewed favorably for girls biologically.

Another reason can be that most male members desire the marriage of their sisters and daughters to maintain their moral status in the community. Because a girl who stays single for a bit longer is seen with suspicion in those societies. People in her immediate vicinity question her honor, doubting her for possible illicit relationships and other health issues. Every father and other male family elders want their daughters and sisters to get married in their early twenties, or occasionally between the ages of fifteen and twenty, to avoid those societal critics.

However, if members of those communities adhere to genuine cultural and true Islamic principles. They will undoubtedly alter how they treat their daughters and sisters and offer them the social privileges they deserve. For instance, in some big cities of Afghanistan, in the past, especially from the early 1930s through the 1980s, girls had the option to decide if they wanted to marry or pursue their education. Girls' education and access to numerous social rights were outlawed with the regime changes of the 1990s, like the Taliban's rise to power. This was caused by the Taliban's strongly religious fundamentalist ideologies, which are at odds with the authentic teachings of the Quran and are more often inspired by certain sects under Islamic titles. For example, banning girls' education.

This is the reason behind the widespread misuse of religion and cultural norms for personal gain. Misusing those principles concerning females makes girls more susceptible to mental health issues. For instance, girls are often unable to speak for themselves when the male family members or parents are in control of their thoughts and hearts and make decisions about how those girls should live and behave.

Therefore, the girls lose their analytical abilities in case of no mental freedom. As a result, those females cannot understand even their most basic rights. Because family members exploit religious and cultural norms, those females become victims of the family's code of conduct. Such mistreatment may also result from male family members' actions toward their daughters and sisters, which are motivated by preserving their societal honor.

Sadly, the situation may also lead to those women sacrificing their lives. Numerous mental conditions may cause their demise. Women may develop depression, for instance, due to the severe psychological damage brought on by their families' inappropriate and utilitarian behavior. Unfortunately, many people, who lack enough knowledge of religion, refer to this depression as a supernatural occurrence.

For instance, they believe that when a lady experiences depression, demons or Jinn must have entered her body or spirit. The local Mullahs even confirm this assertion. The local Mullahs support this assertion for their own religious business to continue. Because when a woman has depression, her family members believe she is keeping Jinn, so they contact their local Mullah. The Mullah then approaches and attempts to remove the Jinn from the victim woman's spirit using certain Arabic words. Psychologically challenged, many women catch several mentally hazardous diseases, and thus those diseases often cause them to die.

SECTION – C.
HAZARDOUS SOCIETY

Are teenagers mentally satisfied with the society they live in? The question is addressed in this section. The section also clarifies the social causes of teenagers' low mental satisfaction and the typical social circumstances that agitate their minds. For this, I pen down tales and offer possible answers based on the conducted research, personal observation, and my understanding of the problems raised. However, these solutions might only apply to some, as everyone has a different outlook and way of life. There are three subsections in this section, the first of which addresses the query, are teenagers satisfied? The social elements that lead to mental enslavement and distress are discussed in the second sub-section, and how teens' thoughts and behavior are used for various objectives is covered in the third sub-section.

Societal Codes

"Don't be satisfied with stories, how things have gone with others. Unfold your myth."
– Rumi, The Essential Rumi

TEENAGERS' HAPPINESS AND mental peace are undermined by various societal variables, both materialistic and non-materialistic. I only discuss the non-materialistic aspects, though, because they significantly affect the ability of teenagers to be mentally content and at peace with themselves. Socially accepted attitudes that contribute to damaging youngsters' mental well-being are to blame for this phenomenon, which is therefore inevitable.

Let us now discuss my interpretation of the quote written above. The quote emphasizes the importance of having personal beliefs, characteristics, and aptitude for independent thought. It is infrequent to find teenagers from undeveloped nations, especially those in the South Asian region like Afghanistan, having the freedom to decide their way of life in their own. This trait significantly impacts a teen's social, familial, and private lives. It can consequently have a larger spectrum of mental impacts.

In such societies in Afghanistan, teenagers typically adhere to the values and customs passed down to them over time. They credit their forebears for following such ideas, viewing them as a sign of respect for traditional norms. Therefore, the illumination of youths' minds and logic is prohibited from innovative ideas by those commonly accepted beliefs. These teens have such constrained perceptions that they cannot consider ideas outside of the norm, which causes them to follow orders or requests of elders without questioning them. Additionally, kids need to consider whether their actions are right or wrong as they practice behavior they have learned from their surroundings, such as parents, peers, and friends. Teenagers impulsively heed what is being done, spoken, or preached by those around them, whether to follow cultural norms or religious principles.

Teenagers' tendency to slavishly adhere to social taboos harms their inner peace and mental fulfillment. Because adhering to such commonly accepted beliefs prevents teens from having the option to think critically, reason, or dispute. As a result, those teenagers' personalities are likewise impacted. Because their mindsets are formed, they must observe and follow their surroundings, elders, classmates, friends, etc., before making any decisions to determine whether it is appropriate to conduct such behaviors.

Additionally, teens would want to confirm that the course of action the teens intend to pursue does not conflict with any cultural or religious traditions. This is because their capacity for decision-making depends on others; their personality is shaped by the acts and behaviors of others. Other people's opinions shape and direct their thoughts. Their entire existence is dictated by what other people want. And eventually, instead of having their ideas, teens begin voicing the words of others.

This behavior is because these kids' brains are rigidly fixed on the idea that accepting to please or satisfy others is acceptable regardless of how harmful it is for their mental well-being. They think that this type of attitude is either supported by cultural standards or a religious precept. Additionally, they believe that social conventions and widely held ideas are appropriate regardless of any evidence to the contrary. This is because disobeying such ideas that are associated with religious principles or occasionally societal rules causes people to fear the horrifying divine punishment.

On the other hand, we frequently encounter clever adolescents who approach every situation with reasoning. However, such teenagers defy accepting social norms, and many others in society may also defy adhering to their beliefs. Those adolescents constantly challenge or question societal beliefs while debating them and presenting rational arguments. Conversely, society defends its position by using religion and culture as shields. However, even religion stresses the use of rationality and opposes such ideas. Here the main issue lies with the dwellers of society that misuse religious principles. Let us use Islam as an example, which urges its adherents to utilize reason before adopting any doctrine, tenet, or custom.

- Tell them that this is my way which is noticeably clear and straight. My call is based on firm conviction, reason, knowledge, and understanding – mine as well as that of my followers. (12:108)

This verse from the Holy Qur'an proves that religion encourages the application of reason and knowledge rather than merely accepting social norms and practices as accurate. Furthermore, there are numerous other passages and al-hadith that strongly emphasize knowledge acquisition and the usage of rationale.

The preceding verse also amplifies the necessity and opportunity of realizing the unity and glory of the Creator. By this we can infer that it's crucial to instill in youngsters the value of knowledge. According to a hadith, the Prophet PBUH once said that the worship of an educated man is far superior to that of an ignorant worshipper (Mustadrak Al-Hakim). This can be accomplished by tilting a reasonable reflection on the cosmos and nature to consider the splendors of God while standing for prayer. In another hadith, The Prophet claims to have declared, "An hour of reflection is better than a hundred years of devotion without reflection." (Al- Bayhaqi)

The entanglement between such true concepts and societal beliefs is detrimental to a teen's mental well-being. It hinders his capacity to consider developing his identity and future. This is because a teen is raised with the idea that he should merely follow society and conform to what others do. Then, societal values influence the personality and actions of that teen. A youngster may secretly contemplate his dreams, which may seem unattainable. Because he is afraid of the danger involved in forging his path, creating his tale, and developing a unique personality that will be different from societal norms.

Finally, he decides to let go of his goals to win over others and accepts that what others do is always correct. And as a result, all the youths in these societies share the same life experiences, character traits, and philosophies. Advancement and bringing about constructive change are therefore impossible. Because they are afraid to confront such innovative views, even though doing so would be detrimental to the future of the youth who live in such communities and the future of the next generation.

To further elaborate on the subject, let us discuss the two main components that are essential for a teenager to deal with. These elements also have an impact on a teen's inner content. These components answer the section's central argument, answering whether teenagers are mentally satisfied with their society.

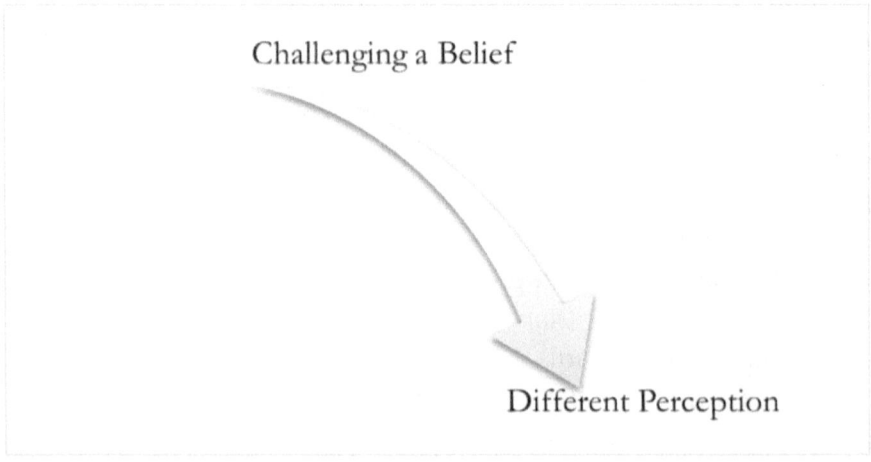

Figure 4. Challenging social codes & disparity in perceptions

Challenging a Belief:

Teenagers in backward societies frequently reach a moment where there is no other course of action except to challenge deeply held beliefs as they become mentally exhausted from sticking to them. However, it is technically cumbersome to disagree with a concept or notion in a culture when individuals of that culture would rather starve to death than abandon or see a backlash to their beliefs. One of the most extensive problems in the backward communities is the widespread cultural taboo that supports the difference between who is right and who is wrong based on age.

Per such taboo, the younger generation must follow the established societal conventions. Teenagers must comply with these conventions and become what society demands and what their elders decide and want them to be. Even if teenagers are correct, they are restricted by social standards from questioning the elders of their family and society because teenagers are considered too young and immature to challenge the beliefs of others. According to mainstream cultural norms, teenagers should not go against their elders and social norms; otherwise, it is rude.

However, this practice is detrimental to youngsters' mental health, especially for those with sharp minds. Since they occasionally desire to pursue their dreams but are compelled by cultural norms to follow the aspirations of their parents, elders, and other socially accepted norms. This behavior frequently keeps these teens from achieving their goals and makes them reliant on the decisions of others.

This is solely the outcome of their elders' authoritarian attitudes, obstinate behavior, and concern with superstitious ideas. Elderly people act more stubbornly towards society than their teens. Those elders worry about social stigma and backbiting that could damage their social reputation if their children do not go with the societal race.

Therefore, it is also possible that teenagers are considered disobedient if they do not follow their elders' desires by adhering to societal norms. In today's date, there is a societal race in which kids are vulnerable to the mental torture of getting no self-esteem and emotional support in society and the family. This is because the respect given to teens in society is often mainly based on their complacent behavior to any conventional belief or performance in school exams. Therefore, getting good grades has become a crucial part of the social race for teens to make their parents feel proud and be ahead of every other kid – even this cost them their peace.

That is why the weightage of scores in a school exam decides the magnitude of respect a teenager receives. Because getting a higher score is something that makes parents feel proud and satisfied, irrespective of how tough it is for some kids to do so. This perception results in the top rank holders of a class getting more respect than the ones with less score, regardless of how intelligent, respectful, and ethical the less score-holder is. Due to such an attitude, many elders need help differentiating between a child's mainstream success and mental satisfaction. Although, elders should understand that the latter is more important. Therefore, a child's most significant success is having a satisfied mind and inner peace rather than being ahead of other kids in a mainstream social race.

This is why most kids in our societies strive to get higher scores, irrespective of whether they practically learn and understand the basic concepts. Many teens, therefore, waste their valuable time by pressurizing themselves to get high scores just to impress their family, elders, and society - such behavior of teens usually costs them their mental peace. Their family elders and the teachers also give more attention to their children and students' scorecards while sidelining their mental satisfaction and other dreams in life. Those parents and teachers forget that prioritizing a child's mental health is equally important as their physical health and grades. Since mental health is invisible, and difficult for the outside world to realize its value.

Let me put down my personal example of defying a belief disguised as a religious obligation. From my childhood age, I have been defying and challenging superstitious beliefs and cultural taboos. I always believed in reality, my dreams, and God-gifted abilities. I neglected what others thought of me or wanted me to do what they deemed was right for me. Even if I did, it would have been as if I had buried my dreams and worked to achieve the dreams of others.

Not only me, but one of my best friends whose mindset resembled mine also faced the same situation. Society and his elders tried several ways to make him follow what they expected. They even tried emotionally extorting him using religious principles and cultural codes. But he remained tenacious in his stance, argued, and then logically proved that no religion and actual cultural values favor any kind of superstitious beliefs. He successfully challenged social beliefs because he had gained enough knowledge about authentic cultural codes, religious principles, and the history of social norms.

According to my friend, that kind of forceful application of norms and beliefs was merely his elders' and society's stubbornness inclined by their satisfaction. This means that society wanted to make my friend follow the status quo, and his elders wanted to victimize my friend's dreams for their pleasure. The elders consider the complacent behavior of teens a sort of obedience and respect for them. And to show off to society how obedient their kids are while destroying their kids' inner happiness.

That type of behavior of teens satisfies their elders' ego, while the elders do not realize that they are doing away with those teenagers' inner peace. I consider this "the death within" for humans, particularly teenagers. The concept of "the death within" applies specifically to those teenagers that are introverted and polite and prioritize respecting others over their inner content, even with the cost of their peace of mind. However, such complacent behavior has always been harmful to teens' inner peace for a lifetime.

In my friend's case, he was brilliant and brave from an early age. However, as he was getting older simultaneously, his behavior also changed. The reason behind this was evident. In his childhood, he was told by his teachers that he, as a kid, was obliged to stay faithful to social norms and the footprints of his elders without questioning them to know whether those footprints were right or wrong. This behavior, which I consider "blind faith," is rationally wrong since it is more like controlling and exploiting kids' minds for personal satisfaction. If I had a little power, I would have sued those people for such behavior – I simply call it barbaric oppression of children's rights – and playing with their innocence, politeness, and loyalty.

This has been the case with every other teenager in Afghanistan who belongs to communities like my friend, and I grew up in. After my friend and I were enrolled in our village Masjid to learn the Holy Quran from our Masjid's Imam or in our local language, "Mullah." At that time, I was around nine years old, and my friend was seven years old. Teenagers at such ages can easily be brainwashed and deceived, though, particularly by using superstitious beliefs disguised as religious obligations coupled with emotionally induced stories of ancient Muslim warriors.

One day, while reciting the Holy Quran in our Masjid, my hat (considered sacred and compulsory to wear as a student of the Holy Quran) suddenly slid off my head. As it hung on my shoulder, I did not care and continued reciting the Holy Quran. However, my friend beside me asked me several times to wear the hat back, but I just left his words unnoticed. Then, after I was called during my turn to learn the new lesson, I stood up and walked towards the Mullah.

While walking, my friend and the Mullah noticed that I did not have my hat on, and the sleeves of my pants (local shalwar kameez) were below my ankles. The Mullah asked me with his stern voice, and eyes turned red that anyone who recites the Holy Quran without having a hat on will taste the torment of the tomb and be thrown into hell. He further added that my pants' sleeves were below my ankles, so for that reason, God would burn my feet in hellfire in the hereafter. He further added that for someone whose pants' sleeves were below his ankles, no Muslims should greet and shake hands with him.

Although I was terrified by the Mullah's remarks as I was a little kid, surprisingly, on the very next day, I saw our Mullah greeting and shaking hands with his brother - who was a college student, and not only were his pants sleeves below his ankles but also, he did not have a hat on his head. I was shocked and remained steadfast for a while, thinking that the same Mullah was scaring me off the hellfire and torment of the tomb on the previous day. He also warned others not to greet me and that no one should shake hands with me for my pants' sleeves below my ankles. I had thought this was a valid and obligatory religious principle that I must have followed. For this reason, I neither greeted nor shook hands with some of my friends whose pants' sleeves were below their ankles. Now I embarrassingly feel regret for that.

Nonetheless, after witnessing our Mullah's discriminatory and dubious behavior, I realized that such people, with such a religious legitimacy, could easily impose their beliefs on ordinary people - predominantly the illiterate and those with little knowledge of religion - as well as those who would never dare to ask such questions because they consider them blasphemy and sensitive. These Mullahs mostly do this to psychologically enslave ordinary individuals to make them obey their teachings to maintain authority over others and earn a tiny bit of wealth. The reason for a scenario like this is apparent. They have already taken control of people's thoughts via cultural rules and taboos or disguised religious beliefs. As a result, people are afraid to question the legitimacy of such fabricated beliefs and practices.

On observing those incidents, I wanted to question our Mullah for his religiously inclined discriminative behavior. I wanted to do this because Mullahs hold a special status in our society and are considered sacred people, which is why everyone respects them. Being socially respected, such discriminative behavior was never expected of him. So, I consulted with my friend first, as I thought this issue looked sensitive. Although he already knew the whole incident, he stopped me from questioning our Mullah.

Nevertheless, I persisted in asking the Mullah. Upon asking him about his discriminative behavior towards me and his brother. He denied answering my question and expressed the reason for his denial by claiming that questioning religious people like a Mullah is a besetting sin which was again a false claim. Meanwhile, my friend warned me that if we continued to upset the Mullah with our questions, he might issue a fatwa against us, and the community — including fellow students at the masjid — could turn hostile, perhaps even resorting to violence.

After hearing this, I was afraid and refrained from further questioning the Mullah, since for those killing, it would be a reward if they killed me for raising questions over a religious master, Mullah. There are many such incidents where people, who have questioned Mullahs, have been lynched by people without knowing the actual reason and the reality. For instance, in 2015, Farkhunda Malikzada, a twenty-seven-year-old Afghan woman, was allegedly lynched by a mob in the capital city of Kabul in Afghanistan due to a false accusation made by a Mullah, blaming her for burning the Holy Quran.

Her only fault was that she reasoned with a Mullah sitting beside a famous masjid called Shah-Do Shamshira in Kabul. However, later the police discovered that she had not done so and that she was utterly authentic and righteous. Unfortunately, she was no longer alive. The Afghan history chronicled this incident as one of the tragic incidents. Thus, based on such life-threatening incidents, my friend was scared we might also face an issue like this. Therefore, we both went near the Mullah and sought apologies fearing that we might face the same fate as Farkhunda.

Nonetheless, my stubborn behavior did not cooperate with my decision. I still asked the Mullah why he did not refuse to greet his brother despite his pants' sleeves being below his ankles. While, the previous day, he had strongly warned me of the hellfire for the same action. He was shocked by my guts for questioning Mullah, and his face turned red, which clearly expressed how angry my behavior had made him. Surprisingly, his response was very unexpected. He responded with a soft tone that one should not question a Mullah, as he would be punished hereafter for such blasphemy behavior. The Mullah considered himself a religious scholar. In Islam, scholars hold immense respect, and the Holy Quran praises knowledge on several occasions. This is the reason many ordinary people respect Mullahs.

Most of the Mullahs, when inquired about such sensitive issues, claim that Muslims are not supposed to question or reason with Mullahs. However, Islamic teachings and the Holy Quran emphasize the use of logic and intellect. This fact shows how the Mullahs always downplay most of the Islamic teachings. Unlike their perspective, our holy Prophet PBUH before his prophecy also used to meditate and question the socially accepted beliefs followed at that time in that area. Even in the Holy Quran, the Almighty says,

"In the creation of the heavens and the earth, and the alternation of night and day, there are signs for people with intelligence, those who remember God standing, sitting, and lying on their sides, and reflect on the creation of the heavens and the earth, (saying) "Our Lord! You have not created all this in vain (Without purpose), Glory is to You. (3:190-91, 7:176, 10:24, 13:3, 16:11).

In conclusion, certain individuals, elites, and the religious masters such as Mullahs, often mix superstitious and man-made societal beliefs with true religious principles to prioritize those societal beliefs over rationale and logic. This is concerning because it creates an environment where superstitious beliefs can thrive over rationale, leading to widespread public ignorance and blind faith. Thus, it can be difficult to challenge these beliefs due to their mainstream nature. Still, it is vital to prioritize critical thinking and logical reasoning coupled with learning true religious principles to combat this phenomenon.

The Difference in Perception:

The difference in perceptions can occasionally result in protracted disagreements, let alone harming a person's mental health. Conflicts between people can spread from their private lives to their families, friend circles, and society. Each person's way of thinking contributes to the difference in their perception from that of others. His capacity to think critically about issues, circumstances, or a phenomenon. The capacity to think critically and ask why, what, and who - is frequently the result of logical reasoning and a person's behavior of curiosity.

Curious people are obsessed with understanding things rather than merely following. Therefore, they always ask questions, and before they ask, they contemplate. They try to learn the answers to their questions, which either helps them learn the desired answers or prompts them to ask new questions. This process of questioning is repeated in a cycle that begins with contemplation, moves on to reasoning, asking questions, seeks answers, and then asking new questions.

Figure 5 illustrates this cycle. The circle keeps recurring with a person's inquisitive activity of inquiring, thinking, and reflecting. Ultimately, this behavior still stems from a person seeing things differently from how others see things. Because while everyone in society abides by the same rules and customs, a person with a different viewpoint can continue living his life as he pleases. And this, as I just stated, may cause conflicts, and impair a person's ability to feel mentally satisfied and content. Because he chooses his own path over society.

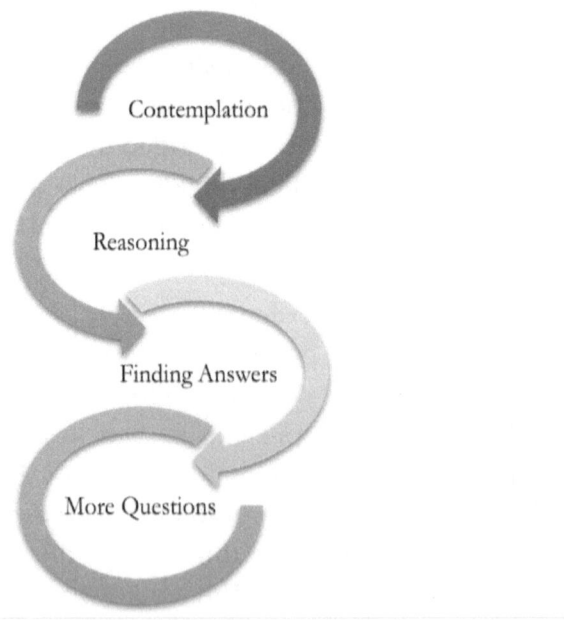

Figure. 5 The Psychological cycle of questioning

Contemplation:

Contemplation is the act of thinking carefully or ruminating about things like a person, place, or situation with in-depth and extensive thoughts. Therefore, contemplation can be the result of a variety of causes. For instance, if a person is unhappy, he is likely to overthink the causes of his melancholy. Numerous ideas may therefore cross his mind.

For example, while thinking, that person may consider holding his friends, his personal life challenges, his dubious future, his family situation, or the societal norms accountable for his mental distress. Based on every individual's personality, people have different thoughts and perspectives. That is what distinguishes the thoughts of one person from another.

Some people frequently like to think about things in calm surroundings. Since introspective thoughts always occur when a person is alone and maintains tranquility. Thinking through problems and producing solutions is much simpler when one is calm. However, many people decide to reflect on a specific topic at night, particularly just before falling asleep while lying in bed. It is a widely held idea in places like Afghanistan that people can think clearly while lying in bed just before sleeping.

However, in the West, people often brainstorm to produce innovative solutions. Brainstorming may seem mentally disturbing to some people, especially those from nations who make decisions based on emotions. This is because people from those backgrounds like to think in a peaceful setting to ponder about a particular issue. Since brainstorming pressurizes one's mind to think quickly and innovatively, it could seem mentally disturbing to those people.

Simply put, contemplation is a type of meditation and self-exploration that can be an acceptable strategy to calm a suffering mind. While discussing contemplation, many people straightaway think about thinking in silence. But we must understand that there is a clear distinction between thinking and silence. I write about thinking since it is a process that has meaning in creating scenarios and finding solutions to problems. While silence is merely a state of tranquility that might not allow us to introspect but is just a way of relaxation.

Reasoning:

Based on my subjective opinion, reasoning comes right after contemplation. Simply said, reasoning is the skill of inquiring about situations. A person thinking about anything discovers a gap in the form of questions that should be filled with the necessary answers just after reaching a certain degree of cognition. He starts asking questions and using logic to produce the desired solutions. That person develops doubts regarding questionable situations during this procedure.

Once more, that particular person still thinks differently. Because he has a unique perspective from the majority of people. With a new outlook, he begins to consider things from an unfamiliar perspective. With a flurry of thoughts racing through his head, he also begins to doubt some socially accepted beliefs.

That person acquires both friends and foes while going through this procedure. In this context, friends are those with the same mentality as that person himself with questions. Individuals who discover such a person to have an unexpectedly different attitude, and one that goes against socially accepted ideas, are considered foes to that person. Even most often, that person is viewed as a dreadful sinner for disagreeing with widely held beliefs, regardless of their correctness.

Though many of the questions of that person are answered, he may have more questions as he digs into the ocean of reasoning. This behavior might be detrimental to one's peace of mind. Because he simply over-pressurizes the mind to logically reason on everything. While anything that is done beyond the limits of one's ability to tolerate becomes poison for them - irrespective of how good that thing is.

Finding Answers:

Curiosity always results in uniqueness and significantly increases our knowledge. Giving more time to studying and reading makes the growth of knowledge possible. An individual may clear up many doubts through research and study given that exploring and researching focus on discovering new things, whether they were invented for the first time or already existed but are being discovered for the first time.

Answering questions can be done through self-exploration, a crucial way to clear doubts. Self-exploration is the process of accepting oneself for who one is – or, to put it another way, loving oneself the way one naturally is. A person drowns in the sea of thoughts in his unlimited yet constrained, vacuuming mind throughout this process. He eventually reaches a place where he discovers the solutions to his problems.

During this process, again, people have different outlooks and perspectives. For instance, some people simply skip their questions without finding appropriate answers. While some other people are stubborn in finding answers to their questions. In the case of the former, the intellectual ability of those people is constrained by societal beliefs. They are mentally enslaved by those commonly accepted norms that prevent such people from thinking cohesively to find answers to their questions.

In the latter's case, those people always seek answers to their questions by pondering things. These people see themselves as psychologically free from mainstream beliefs or norms, which is also why such people always have questions.

More Questions:

Finally, after discovering the satisfactory answers to a particular inquiry, a person reaches a point where he frequently starts to have more questions. These only appear to be questions that have been taken from answers to the previous questions. Those answers of that person continue to generate more questions. This phenomenon tempts the person to restart the procedure from the beginning. The person, therefore, begins to have doubtful thoughts resulting in contemplation, reasoning, finding answers, & having more questions. During this cycle, however, a person learns a lot from new experiences and aspects of life.

Adding to the research and found discoveries also contributes to this process. As a researcher's questions are the reason for conducting research in the first place. Nevertheless, the person continues to gather additional facts and literature while seeking solutions. In the form of doubts, this technique leaves a vacuum. For example, atheist skeptics frequently question religious people on the existence of God. Similar inquiries frequently spark further questions. The respondents to such questions muse on how to address the query on how to prove God's existence. Even if they do respond that response will more likely be inspired by the socially accepted belief, which may need to be more satisfactory. This question, therefore, begs more questions by encouraging debates over this topic.

Nonetheless, one reason behind a perpetual succession of the creation of questions is the lack of relevant scientific and religious knowledge by both parties – the one who asks and the one who responds. The existence of God could be both religiously and scientifically proven. Still, it is possible that the person who favors religion may not be ready to accept scientific theories or laws. While the one who is on the side of science may refuse to accept any religious principle.

As a result, the process of self-discovery then begins. For instance, questions about God, humankind, the universe, etc., encourage people to examine themselves. A person tends to have many questions, answers, and more questions after self-exploration and pondering sensitively mysterious questions and events. This approach occasionally even questions social norms. When social ideas are questioned, people attempt to alter how others perceive them through education and other means to support their claims and ensure they can tell the difference between true and untrue.

Overall, my practical experience and observation have shown that differences in perception frequently result in three fundamental factors that, in my opinion, hinder a person's mental content: For instance, comparing one's life to that of others which may be typically harmful to one's emotional well-being by way of suffering from an inferiority complex. Usually, society also makes comparisons like this. Inclined by such societal beliefs, elderly people in middle-class families, for example, are merely happy with their children's accomplishments, regardless of how tough fulfilling those accomplishments might be for their children. They disregard their teens' wishes, happiness, and choices, nevertheless.

This way, teenagers get extorted using distorted cultural values and societal norms if they disobey the advice of their elders or relatives. Teenagers, therefore, become entangled in a conundrum as a result of such behavior of their family elders. Teens get trapped between their desires and happiness and societal expectations and conventions. Teenagers who are mentally imprisoned end up suffering from mental anguish and dissatisfaction. They worry about being judged negatively by society for breaking social norms and codes.

The Bottom Line:

Overall, today's many teenagers seem to be mentally dissatisfied with the society in which they live. The reason remains the forceful psychological involvement in the enforced societal race. While today's generation has access to information technology, they are far more aware about events than prior generations. Because they are growing up in a different period than the prior generation.

The temporal difference between today's generation and the preceding one makes it difficult for teenagers to live according to their wants while meeting society's expectations. Because everyone has a unique perspective, everyone should be allowed to make decisions about their lives. Regardless of their particular viewpoints, everyone nowadays feels compelled to adopt the same societal belief system.

Furthermore, teenagers with brilliant minds, in particular, are more susceptible to such environments. Because their attitude is inherently receptive to innovative ideas and out-of-the-box critical thinking. However, they are mentally coerced to adhere to a fixed set of pre-programmed codes. Such a coded belief system is pre-determined and pre-decided, implying that there is no place for out-of-the-box thinking and that every individual must think in a pre-determined manner. Teens need clarification about what and how to think, say, and do, owing to religious principles, cultural conventions, and subjective opinions.

Psychological Enslavement

PSYCHOLOGICAL ENSLAVEMENT, AS per my personal experience, refers to the mental condition of an individual wherein his thoughts, actions, decisions, and opinions are controlled by the thoughts, actions, decisions, and opinions of others. In other words, mental enslavement is the process of influencing other people's thoughts, opinions, and decisions. Or having own thoughts, opinions, and decisions been influenced by the behavior of other people. In the first case, one mentally controls others, whereas, in the latter case, other people mentally control that person. Thus, mental enslavement is mentally controlling other people or being mentally controlled by them.

Mental enslavement mainly occurs during the age group of nine to twenty years. In simple words, it occurs during the teenage years. However, teenagers are mainly mentally enslaved by societal norms or family behavior at this age. While in some rare cases, they tend to mentally enslave others of the same age group – mostly their peers, ones in acquaintance, or those younger than them. For acquaintances, making them emotionally dependent on you and then blackmailing them for a variety of purposes is the most efficient method of manipulating their minds.

For example, when children crave toys or snacks, they mostly make emotional stories of comparisons referring to their friends, saying, "Look at Ahmad whose mother always buys him whatever he asks for, and you never buy me anything I wish." This way, the child indirectly controls his mom's mind by extorting her to fulfill his desires. We can call this the child's mental enslavement of his mom because the mom is emotionally attached to her child.

There are ample other similar instances that highlight the phenomenon of mental enslavement quite clearly. These instances include personal, social, and family issues. However, here I focus on social factors that cause mental enslavement. Among those are the socially accepted beliefs that cause a significant deterrence to a teen's mental peace.

This deterrence results in an individual being mentally enslaved by society through those mainstream beliefs. Since my focus is more on backward communities where people pay substantial attention to religion-based principles and societal beliefs or codes. This majorly happens regardless of any specific attention to the other side of the coin. We need to understand the flip side of the coin as to how the exploitation of such codes and their manipulation with fallacious beliefs harm the mental peace or satisfaction of the young generation.

For example, today's teenagers have access to smartphones and the Internet. For parents, diverting from traditional life to being captivated by virtual life is detrimental to their children's mental health. However, the use of internet may not be as harmful to teenagers' mental health as the mental anguish they endure due to social stigma, or the severe restrictions parents use to prevent their children from using the Internet. The approaches used by parents to prevent their children from using the Internet are vital. This is determined by the level of comprehension of parents and children and their communication routes in mind.

Understanding and communication between parents and their children are critical for resolving such issues. Parents may be unable to adequately convey a message to their children if they have common understanding and communication gaps. As a result, parents must have a sense of humor and learn how to communicate with their children.

Here, too, society has a part. Assume a teenager uses a cell phone and a villager observes him singing or dancing on the street. That villager may not be at ease because the boy is too young to listen to a song or dance, which goes against the prevailing social scale of respect. Villagers may contact the boy's parents to seize his phone and advise him not to sing or dance publicly. In this case, the villagers attempt to uphold their socially driven ego by assuming they restore traditional norms while imposing those norms on the boy.

However, to better explain the point, let us refer to the case of Mullahs. Mullahs are used as an example since they have a significant role in Afghan society. They are revered from the religious angle and in the cultural sector of Afghan society.

Aside from Mullahs, community, and village leaders are another vital group in shaping many far-flung Afghan societies, also known as village elders in rural Jorgen. The behavior of village elders could also psychologically imprison youngsters, mainly through cultural codes and conventions. They do this primarily to accomplish whatever they desire – probably the power to control villagers and retain social status. Also, to make teenagers follow them without questioning or arguing. This behavior offers older people feelings of gloating and satisfaction.

For instance, in many villages in Afghanistan, tribal feuds sporadically take place due to several reasons. Usually, this chain of tribal feuds has now become somewhat of a cultural tradition in far-flung small villages. Surprisingly, many a time, people even considered continuing feudal enmity as an honor for the culture and a sign of might. For example, taking revenge on one's loved ones is still considered bravery.

Taking revenge, however, gives the involved party the feeling of satisfaction. At the same time, the other side of this coin is different and miserable. Taking revenge can also lead to the other person's willingness to take back revenge. As a result, the chain of taking revenge lasts longer and for years, decades, and even centuries from generations to generations. This enmity then reaches a point where members of all the involved parties either get killed or migrate from the place of their origin.

On the other hand, fortunately, many broad-minded and educated teenagers in Afghanistan vehemently oppose such practices. They believe that such practices are perilous to people's lives – not just their mental peace. Therefore, they claim that anything harmful to human life must be washed away. Nonetheless, they continuously get extorted by the elites with fallacies disguised as cultural codes and beliefs.

Not only have feudal disputes wrecked the true Afghan cultural norms, but also several other issues. For instance, those issues emerge due to disagreements over the ownership of a piece of land or conflicts over each family's turn of irrigational water to irrigate their crops. Thus, when educated teenagers oppose adhering to such codes, they are forced into mental enslavement by extorting them with fallacious beliefs.

The elites and elders do this by giving them a touch of cultural and religious values just to have the teenagers follow them to restore the traditions left out in perpetual succession from the previous generations. This norm will result in the wreckage of both the true religious and cultural codes of conduct as well as the mental peace of youth.

For this kind of mental enslavement of teenagers, various techniques are used. For example, as stated above, among those techniques is emotional blackmailing, and elites along with other elders supporting their claim with cultural codes and values. These two approaches are the two primary methods elites use to have their voices heard by the teenagers so that they do what they are asked to do. For instance, many people consider taking revenge in feudal conflicts a cultural norm – which is absolutely antipathetic to the true cultural codes.

However, this practice is not as it is socially touted – but utterly an antipathetic practice to the authentic cultural codes. Still, teenagers are forced to follow it, regardless. The defiance of teenagers to accept such demands arouse their elders' frustration to scold teenagers and forcefully impose their desires. Suppose teenagers still do not wish to accept what their elders want from them. In that case, the elders try to emotionally extort teenagers and make them do so.

This is the main reason why teenagers must learn to control their emotions. If not, their emotions will otherwise control them. I recommend that teenagers control their emotions rather than immediately trying to change mentally perilous societal conventions because emotions are within oneself, whereas norms are external. This means that a person can easily control his emotions, but he cannot possibly control external beliefs.

Social Business:

According to economic and business principles, the greater the need for a product or service, the greater the customer demand for that product or service. Therefore, businessmen and manufacturing firms attempt to generate demand for their products and services by assuring that the target customers require that product or service. As a result, those businesses advertise their products or services primarily to emphasize customers to realize the need for those products and services and thus purchase them.

Companies may purposefully create an unprecedented need by intimidating customers with dire repercussions if they do not purchase and use their products or services. For example, a medicine company. They warn people of prospective diseases if they do not use the medicine of that particular company.

Similarly, the longer patients are unwell, the more doctors will have their businesses run. The more terrorists continue their occupation of terrorism, the more the world's institutes for peacebuilding and promotion will leverage. Similarly, the greater people dread superstitious thoughts, their need for religion increases. The more superstitious beliefs exist, the more some religious merchants will profit from it – which I consider religious business.

Everything is in proportion to the other. This demonstrates how we must not judge people or if we do, our judgement should be based on their social ethics, behavior, and overall personality rather than their personal religious views. Because religion is our personal relationship with God. What matters to others is how we treat them, whether we harm or benefit them. Otherwise, evaluating individuals based on the extent of their worship implies that we are perfect, which we are not, therefore assuming the position of God, which is unjust.

Unfortunately, assessing people based on the number of prayers or acts of devotion they undertake is pervasive in our societies. In many far-flung Afghan villages, the quantity of worship is given more credence than one's level of education, attitude, behavior, or achievements. This demonstrates how people fail to distinguish between religion and culture. God prefers that we be kind to our fellow humans first rather than being evil to humanity while obeying God. Since God forgives if a person forgets to pray, he does not forgive someone who harms other humans until the victim first forgives the culprit.

The same is true for societal norms. The more people are forced to make decisions about their lives based on how others live, the more they are mentally enslaved by the elites in society. Alternatively, the more they make their decisions based on the opinions of others, which is disguised as social standards, the more utilitarian elites and heads will gain from it. Their gain, however, will be both materialistic and non-materialistic. Non-materialistic gains will restore their power over villagers, and materialistic gains will result in more properties and wealth. This is best exemplified by the fact that, the more people blindly adhere to the rules framed by elites, the more the truth will vanish. Because the culture of blind obedience has always been the greatest enemy of truth.

The village leaders often use culture and religion to dominate the villagers' mentality. Once the working class is dominated by the elites and heads, they can no longer make their own life decisions. This syndrome also psychologically affects teenagers. When teenagers notice that their elders' decisions are influenced by the opinions of other villagers or the village elites, they accept it as part of society's standards. As a result, this practice is undisputed and consequently gets ingrained in societal norms.

Even if a teenager, who freely thinks outside of the social race, wishes to defy such standards, surprisingly, the villagers will be the first to oppose the teenager from maintaining those norms. The elites and village leaders will begin to worry about a threat to their authority and dominance over the locals.

As a result, the elites will persuade ordinary folks to oppose that teenager, accusing him of violating social standards and religious precepts. While the role of the local Mullah in such instances is inevitable, he will eventually step onto the ground. He will likely label the teen disobedient, disloyal, rebellious, pagan, or infidel for he goes against the mainstream norms.

The locals sometimes begin violently retaliating against the teenager as soon as the Mullah approves the accusations made by the villagers and elites. Unfortunately, teenagers are more likely to face harsh repercussions as a result. This is why disastrous societal norms have constantly afflicted us, the Pashtuns – especially the young generation.

Emotional Distress

MY PERSONAL EXPERIENCE has shown me that emotional discomfort in teenagers often develops when they are dealing with a fatal mental disease due to some past occurrence or confrontation with people. Multiple reasons contribute to teens having such fragile mental health. However, I primarily concentrate on the social causes of emotional distress in teenagers in this section. Based on my subjective experience of Afghanistan, society and the environment play a significant role in reshaping a person's personality and general outlook on the outside world. Throughout my life, I have identified a few elements that play a vital role in developing emotional stress in teenagers and how that affects their mental health.

The first element is holding onto a series of socially accepted beliefs, notwithstanding how detrimental they are to teenagers' mental health. I have already mentioned this point, however. Teenagers raised in backward environments have perplexing feelings of hesitation while accepting or rejecting specific social ideas. This is because they are stuck in some impasse where they must uphold a never-ending string of conventional wisdom that dates back hundreds of years but is entirely at odds with modern life.

However, today's world requires rationale, education, innovation, insight, and reasoning. While the continuity of such mainstream beliefs is founded on the ancient way of life and the social norms that prevailed hundreds of years ago. As a result, such beliefs are more superstitious in nature given today's dynamic world. They oppose the modern approach of today's world, which demands logic and rationale encouraged by observed facts.

In the majority of the remote areas of Afghanistan, however, people still prioritize cultural taboos over the right to free expression, reason, and a lifestyle that is lived with a free psychological will. Even though they know that they are compromising their ability to live as independent humans, people in certain areas are obligated to adhere to some cultural ideas and beliefs. People who live in such areas are unaware of how the wealthy class takes advantage of their blind faith and convictions with honest intentions.

This is so that no one can stand up for themselves or criticize the elite class since the whole cultural system and lifestyle are set up so - that no one can dare take action. This is because the general social system is constructed to prevent anyone from speaking up for themselves or expressing reasoned criticism of the elite class. However, some decent and educated teens accept to endure the mental anguish of having their voices stifled in those communities. They do so because they merely want to avoid any conflict which can be raised in case of their backlash against societal norms.

The utilitarian behavior of the elite class in those societies and the head of most of the families are the sole reasons for the teenagers' mental distress by keeping the teenagers mentally controlled and enslaved. As much as the middle class in those societies and the teenagers in the families of such societies remain unchanged and strive for a profound revolution to end such hazardous beliefs, those teenagers and middle-class families will end up suffering for the rest of their life. The infliction of this saga will continue to last and harm middle-class families and teenagers forever, unfortunately.

Additionally, mental enslavement coupled with emotional distress causes several other grave issues like long-lasting poverty and corruption. Teenagers are made to do what they are asked to do, especially the things that their ancestors used to do. Since they must adhere to the mainstream cultural norms, teenagers need to do what their elders and the elite class make them do. In case of disobedience, the teenagers are considered impolite and unethical. However, this is considered important for teenagers to safeguard the so-called cultural norms. However, the aftermath of this behavior could be disastrous in the long run for society as a whole.

Livelihood Disparity

Because of the behavior of elites mentioned above, poverty, and corruption may also ensue and increase. For example, when villagers' minds become restricted and confined by mainstream norms, they will remain in a shielding stance. Their sole attempt will be to defend themselves by being respectful and sticking to mainstream norms - whether they want to or not. As a result, villagers cannot even think or speak about their fundamental rights.

This is why many middle-class families end up poor when their freedom to decide and speak is controlled by village elites. The inability to speak about their rights to benefits will likely change the villagers' thinking about fulfilling their needs, such as through illicit means.

As a result of the discrepancy between their lifestyle and that of the elites, there is a risk of illicit acts such as theft by poor villagers. While the middle-class villagers cannot afford the same lifestyle as the elite, they crave and endure living at least half of the elite's lifestyle. Their inner anguish multiplies when they realize they cannot speak up or do anything to improve their standard of living.

In this case, the middle class begins to consider illegal means of obtaining bread, regardless of their legitimacy or damage to society. However, in case of any harm to society by poor villagers, I accuse the elites of such harm. Young boys and girls, like villagers in general, are vulnerable to inner suffering as a result of disparities in livelihood. Such disparity, nonetheless, is justified by elites by using several social norms established by those elites.

One of these norms is the tradition of expensive marriages. An impoverished groom cannot afford the hefty dowry price the bride's parents impose. He may also need help to afford the extravagant wedding expenditures the bride's parents and family recommended. While the bride's family wants to impress society with lavish decorations and expensive wedding luxury, the groom suffers psychologically due to financial constraints.

Once again, practices like these harm impoverished villagers. One question that frequently irritates me is why someone would strive to impress society at the price of their own happiness and the happiness of their loved ones. The reason, however, might be that individuals constantly want to show off and please society, even in reality, if they are not who they appear to be.

The disparity between the life of elites and the destitute villagers may also contribute to sentiments of unworthiness and inferiority complex. Many middle-class teens psychologically suffer from less-worthiness and inferiority complex after seeing the lifestyles of elite teenagers. As a result, to get involved with the mainstream social race of show off, poor teens attempt every reasonable means - as previously indicated - to earn money and create the lifestyle they wish. Instead, to avoid mental suffering, I advise these teens to either avoid such poisonous norms or speak and behave against such norms rather than impressing society.

Thus, rather than comparing their lifestyle to that of the elites, they should be appreciative and satisfied with what they already possess and their stable and modest way of life. Another viable option is to raise public awareness about the importance of standing up to social inequalities disguised as societal codes.

Furthermore, when poor kids feel less worthy of themselves, they build friendships with teenagers from wealthy families. Those wealthy youngsters' lifestyles are far more luxurious than those of the poor ones. Their way of living could be less affordable for poor teenagers. This is why, after making friends with elite households' teenagers, impoverished teens simply harm themselves by being unable to meet the requirements of and match the level of rich teenagers.

As a result, poor teens may resort to illegitimate means of earning money and living to keep up with their wealthy friends. Meanwhile, poor teens develop expectations and trust with their wealthy peers. Ultimately, poor teenagers are more prone to emotional distress if their trust is betrayed, or their expectations are not satisfied. This is what I consider a toxic friendship.

Toxic Friendships

When we wish for wisdom, we start to experience hardships to obtain wisdom from the experience we get via those hardships. The same is true for people who enter our lives and eventually become a significant part of our life. As a result, when we seek mental peace, God first puts toxic people into our lives so that we might recognize them and avoid them in the future. Thereafter we tend to trust less, expect less, and, most importantly, rely less on everyone after living with toxic individuals. As a result, we enjoy mental peace since we are prepared for the worst with less expectations and are not emotionally dependent on individuals who do not appreciate our presence.

While nothing in this world is free, pointless, or useless, everything happens for a reason. Everything that happens to us or anybody who enters our lives has a purpose. Everything that comes to us is in exchange for something that goes away. Thus, God provides something or someone better into our lives when we lose something or someone. To keep a delicate friendship, it is vital to uphold the other party's trust and appreciate their honesty. Otherwise, this world is so cruel, which often makes it difficult for us to find perfect and honest friendships.

Friendship is essential in shaping one's personality during one's youth. What and how a person thinks defines his personality. The way we think is determined by who we associate with. Suppose a person's mental health and personality are harmed if he is focused on his career goals while socializing with people who are careless with their careers and future. It makes no difference how strong our bond is or how close the other person becomes to us; if our mind is not aligned with our friend's, the friendship will not last.

As a result, we may suffer repercussions such as being trapped, mistreated, or hurt. Because a friend with an opposite mindset may drag us to their level and comfort zone, we may be distracted from our main path in life. Even the level of similarity in our standpoint with that of our siblings and close ones is so crucial. So much so if our close ones or siblings have a different mindset, we may not be able to live happily and peacefully with them. The question here is why we still continue to live with our siblings despite the disparity in our mindsets.

In Afghanistan, however, we live together with our siblings in extended families because we are emotionally attached to one another. Afghan cultural values reinforce this emotional bond by encouraging us to live with our siblings so that we all can support one another in times of need - no matter what. It is reasonable, though; there may be disagreements if our mindsets do not match those of our siblings.

To avoid such potential squabbles, we must encourage, tolerate, and accept one another rather than attempt to impose our particular thoughts and views on our siblings. Suppose we believe our younger siblings are misled or doing something wrong. In that case, we are expected to guide them by example rather than telling or advising them. To do this, older siblings must first transform themselves into who they want their younger siblings to be.

This also pertains to who the elder siblings connect with. The social life and friend circle of elder siblings directly impact the outlook of younger siblings on friendship. While younger siblings learn from their elders by observing them, older siblings must make beneficial connections so that their younger siblings are positively influenced and subsequently want to emulate their elders.

Nonetheless, in most Afghan societies, elders often want younger siblings to form friendships with the younger siblings of their friends. For example, a teen may be encouraged to hang out with the younger siblings or sons of his father's or elder brother's friends. This is because younger siblings in certain societies are made to believe that their elders' friends must be trusted and considered decent individuals. After all, their elders maintain connections with them.

This behavior of elders looks more like mental torture than a favor to a teenager. Because mentally forcing a teen to hang out with someone that he may or may not like is mental torture which also causes emotional distress in a teenager. Eventually, the teenager will suffer more than achieve anything by being forced to hang out with people they do not like. Therefore, it is important for elders to let their youngsters decide their friends themselves – yet with friendly and indirect supervision. This way the teenagers will learn from experiencing both positively and negatively.

It could be possible that the siblings of elders' friends have different views and attitudes than that of a teenager. Therefore, the friends of a teenager do not necessarily have to be individuals he already knows or the siblings of those who are friends with the elders of that teenager. But those whose thoughts and understandings are similar to those of that teenager.

In this regard, elders must show their teens to evaluate and choose who they want to befriend. This is possible when elders have decent friend circles. Therefore, elders must first surround themselves with moral and ethical friends to develop the ability of their teens to analyze friendships. This way, those elders may demonstrate and assist their younger siblings in forming friendships with decent and ethical individuals, particularly those with similar viewpoints.

Key Takeaways:

- My experience has convinced me that it is most effective not to value and respect specific individuals more than they deserve. There needs to be a limit to our behavior regarding who we deal with. Because we must connect and deal with people based on their level of understanding. This will protect us from experiencing emotional distress.
- Teenagers should be taught to recognize the significance of similarities in maturity, mentality, and understanding levels with whomever they form friendships. They should also make friendships with those with the same lifestyle and behavior.
- We may not realize it, but our excessively soft and pleasant behavior with some people delights them while causing us

- mental discomfort. We need to change that behavior.
- The minute we quit emotionally relying on individuals who once mattered the most to us, we gain peace of mind because we achieve mental freedom. Our psychological dependency dissipates, and our inner peace and positive mental health become unconditional.
- When you need clarification about the actual personality of your friends, purposefully give them time and value and see how they use your time and respect. You must take charge of your life, decisions, and emotions. Your decisions should be free; your self-esteem, self-respect, and mental peace should be your top priorities. Meanwhile, prioritize your family, parents, and certain loved ones. Before getting familiar with someone, make sure the person is of your level.
- When elders provide unsolicited advice to teenagers, those teenagers frequently get offended - especially in front of people. As a result, rather than simply advising kids what to do or not do, elders should guide them by following the same advice. Because when teens get offended, they lose self-esteem and confidence.
- While everyone has their perspective, life goals, and preferred way of doing things, we should accept them for who they are, what they think and stick to our own path. Therefore, something other than what works for one individual might not work for another. Accepting this fact will benefit our mental health.
- Also, we must always expect less and do more to gain inner content. Because our society has consistently failed to distinguish between prosperity and fulfillment. Therefore, society must recognize that true success is satisfaction, which is always more than anything else.
- When we get emotionally hurt by others, it is better to be alone or with those who share our perspectives and wisdom rather than with the wrong, toxic, and immature people who

cannot understand and feel us.
- Instead of listening to toxic words from the wrong people, I would rather spend my time reading books or doing things that will help me advance my career and get me closer to my goals. The same applies to every teenager. Instead of wasting time listening to unnecessary words, it is better to read, listen to podcasts, watch documentaries, or do anything that helps them build their personality.
- When I am in pain, I would instead write down my feelings on a piece of paper than share them with the wrong people and those who do not value my words. Likewise, I advise every teenager to follow the same. This way they will respect their own feelings by not wasting them on the wrong people.

The Exploitation of Social Status

THE MAJORITY OF far-flung regions in Afghanistan still adhere to a centuries-old, widespread, informal, and socially supported leadership style. This is true both in Afghanistan and in certain Pashtun-populated regions of Pakistan. While observing this type of leadership style, I have understood that it has been practiced indefinitely, which is more of an authoritarian approach.

For instance, the hierarchy of such a leadership style is structured so that it is always expected to be led by one head, who is known as the (Malak) in the local language. The villagers do not elect the head (Malak) of the village but rather select him. The Malak is joined by a small group of other village elders who serve as his counselors. These individuals actively participate and help the Malak with deciding essential village issues.

Malak, the head of every hamlet, is wealthy, powerful, and widely recognized by the local populace. However, the criteria for becoming the Malak (head) of a village is that one does not need to have formal education or be appropriately qualified. Typically, a Malak is chosen by a limited group of other influential village elders who accompany him as his advisors and provide him with guidance and consultation on various village-related matters.

Simply put, the society's leader (Malak) and other villagers pay attention to what those elders say, especially when significant decisions are being made. Everyone believes that because they are elderly, they are intelligent and experienced and that anything they say should be accepted by everyone.

One of the significant elements regarding such a leadership style that is essential to comprehend is the factors on which it bases its entire decision-making process. First, rather than being based on facts or valid reasoning, decision-making is frequently heavily influenced by cultural norms, religious beliefs, and, most frequently, the status quo. Another intriguing aspect of this leadership style's decision-making is the need for more room for logical debate or criticism, particularly between female or younger members and the male elders who also make the decisions.

This is because the elders regard themselves to be the sole decision-makers and reserve all other decision-making authority for themselves. Therefore, the older generation does not like being argued with or questioned about their decisions because they view it as disrespectful to their character and the status that society accords to them.

The issue under discussion at this point is how such a leadership style affects youngsters' mental health. The younger members of society, as well as the female members, are not favored by the older, male-dominated leadership style. Here is how I have documented my experience and observation.

The elders, influenced by their love of and fixation with authority and respect, are also not willing to hear any advice from the younger and female members, no matter how helpful it may be. In addition, it is regarded as unfriendly and disrespectful to the elders, cultural norms, and beliefs when the younger and female members voice their ideas.

Teenagers and female members of society are therefore expected to be quiet and submissive and to follow any laws, beliefs, and codes being put out and decisions made by the elders, regardless of their significance or disadvantage to society. Respecting their elders and presenting themselves as courteous and submissive is a required norm for youths and female members of society.

To me, this behavior corresponds to indirect mental torture. It is upsetting to the feelings of female members and teenagers alike.

Because subscribing to such ideas, which I view as merely superstitious standards, benefits primarily the elderly and those in positions of power rather than ordinary individuals in society. In this way, the elders take advantage of the youth and women's submission and obedience since they gain their respect and status as long as they stay submissive, silent, and occasionally obedient.

Additionally, the village's leader (Malak) takes advantage of the younger people's pliable nature in one way or another. This might be nothing less than enduring emotional pain for teenagers. Because they have no choice but to keep adhering to such a cultural taboo.

Many intelligent, critical-thinking, and mature youth disagree with these notions. These teens are aware of the long-lasting effects of such beliefs. They know they can even refute such beliefs using logic and wisdom. Yet, conservative individuals do not support the bright-minded youth. They are actively hostile toward them in their fight against such superstitious beliefs. At a certain point, those teenagers could also suffer psychologically as a result. They would wish they were unaware of such truths.

It is crucial to comprehend what would result from such views, as I just described, to avoid the consequences of such beliefs. Such beliefs have a lasting effect that extends beyond the precincts of society, neighborhood, or province, finally impacting the entire nation.

First, teenagers tend to develop into physically free yet emotionally and mentally dependent adults who do not look outside the box. They cannot criticize or reason with the elders, even if they are correct. They eventually come to live under mental captivity and slavery. This is because I have seen numerous teenagers debating with their elders and being labeled as disrespectful.

The reason is that they did not follow cultural norms that encouraged children to always obey elders - no matter what. Many kids experience mental pain due to this pernicious cultural taboo, which only serves to exploit them. They eventually reach a point of extreme mental endurance where they either kill themselves or tend to leave the house because they seem to be fed up and have no other choice but to continue living alone.

For teenagers, such a leadership style has other repercussions. For instance, social status exploitation. Teenagers, particularly those from middle-class households, are more susceptible to such a status quo. When their voices are muted, and their feelings are buried within them. Their vulnerability even doubles when they desperately want to express their feelings and speak for themselves. Still, due to societal beliefs, they cannot do so. Their repressed voices become a poison that eats away at their soul and snatches their inner peace. Unfortunately, such anguish can persist longer than intended and result in death. This problem is prevalent in civilizations where culture and religion control people's minds.

The Theft at the Masjid:

During my childhood, I had a close friendship with one of my neighbors, who was about nine years old – a year younger than me, as I recall. As a result of the boy's misbehavior and aggressive actions toward other neighbors, his father and older brothers would frequently beat him. Forcing their children to obey the elders' commands by hitting them was one of the most prevalent yet retrospective habits of the elders living in the area. Despite being frequently beaten by his elders, that boy, my friend, was thoughtful and active in his life routine.

One day the villagers found out that a ceiling fan from the masjid in our village was missing at some point in the wee hours of the morning. Oddly enough, that night, my mischievous friend was not keeping up well and was sleeping all day and all night on his bed. He had to deal with another unanticipated trauma while battling his severe condition. This is because my friend's wicked behavior was already well-known, and it was obvious that he would be held accountable for the losses.

The following morning my friend's life had some unexpected changes, as one of the grey-bearded men, who was a consistent performer of five times a-day prayer - and was regarded as the important masjid custodian, had to handle this issue. The grey-bearded man and my friend had already had several arguments, so it was evident he would blame my friend. The following day after the village masjid held its afternoon prayer, everyone was seated on the prayer mat and waiting for the Imam to pray after Namaz (prayer) when the grey-bearded man mentioned the matter of the missing ceiling fan.

As usual, everyone simply cast suspicion and made rumors about my friend, stating that he was the one who must have taken the fan. Since everyone in the masjid was sure that no one else in the community would ever try to steal the fan from the masjid—which was both unethical and against religious and societal norms—no one dared to even consider such action.

After some muttering and puzzled stares from the people toward one another, they finally exclaimed loudly that the only person who could have performed this crime was that naughty boy—my friend—which saddened me to hear. I could not speak up for him or argue his case, though. But eventually, everyone agreed that he must have taken the fan.

The boy's father was also there in the masjid. After witnessing the entire incident, he dejectedly departed the masjid for his house. When my friend's dad got home, he immediately walked downstairs to my friend's room and, without saying a word, slapped him to release his rage. He then questioned my friend about what had happened. My friend adamantly denied stealing anything from the masjid and claimed that day that he had been ill all day and night. My unruly friend's parents, as well as the rest of the family, believed him because he was unwell and because he was telling the truth.

Surprisingly, the masjid Mullah and those close to him brought up the same issue again the next day after the afternoon prayer. What bothered me? What if the villagers had bought another fan and resolved the issue the day before? I was also wondering why the Mullah wanted the issue to continue. Or he wanted to create drama by blaming an innocent kid from a middle-class family and then jumping in and assuming to help the situation. The locals' respect for the Mullah

THE EXPLOITATION OF SOCIAL STATUS

would rise this way, and everyone would applaud him for resolving the problem.

Therefore, after learning that my friend was ill, the Mullah supported the news of his illness, as he assumed to fix the problem – indeed, but lately. The Mullah did not support my friend's claim for being truthful about not stealing the fan but for being ill – as he still cunningly believed that my friend must have stolen the fan. Nonetheless, shockingly the Mullah kept questioning my friend's ability to steal from the masjid while he was ill. The village leader (Malak) and many of the villagers, however, were not in support of the boy and kept asserting that the masjid's custodian's claim about my friend for stealing the fan was correct. That villager was the one who had first mentioned the problem.

Several days passed, but still, the issue remained unresolved. When the boy finally recovered, he went outside to play cricket with us. We were so happy seeing him among us on the playground after several days. We were so curious to know the actual story and determine if he had stolen the fan or was he innocent. After we finished playing cricket, we all inquired him about the issue. He was close to us, so we understood he would not mind us asking him about this issue.

At first, he did not want to say anything about the issue as he said nobody would believe him, and he also said that despite swearing multiple times, everyone kept doubting him. He said he was weary of trying to prove himself innocent – as nobody believed him. After several attempts, he firmly swore by Allah that he had not stolen the masjid fan.

We already believed him by realizing his absence from the cricket game for a few days due to his illness. So, we were sure that he had not stolen the fan. That was why we promised him our full support and assured him that he did not have to worry. Nonetheless, he had already been stressed out and depressed. His depression went as high as we noticed that he had black circles around his eyes due to such severe depression. But everyone in our friend circle was terrified as my friend looked tense.

While on the way back home, he said that he got beaten up very severely by his dad as his dad was angry, not because of his thoughts about the stolen masjid fan but because he had to listen to the villagers' stigma about his son. Thus, to release his frustration of hearing the villagers' stigma, his dad had no option except to beat up his son. The boy told us that his neck was hurting severely since his dad had flogged his neck with a stick.

That evening, all of us friends sat with him in front of our masjid for longer than usual. Everyone was so sad, especially after we saw the scars on his neck caused by the stick whips – as his dad had whipped him with a stick. The following morning our doorbell rang continuously for several moments. My mom awoke me to check the door since I was the youngest of our family's male members, and I had to do such microtasks. As I rushed to the door, it was pretty early in the morning; I first sneaked across the door and then looked through the small hole in the door hinge. I was shocked to see my friend's dad standing, nervous and panicked, behind the door. This made me feel frightened to see my friend's dad panicking.

I opened the door anyway, and before I could say anything, he suddenly started speaking and asked if I knew where his son was. I had no idea, though, and I had no words to respond to him with either. However, I sadly expressed my sympathy and promised to help him find his missing son – my friend. Later I realized that his son had been missing since last night – the night we met him after playing cricket. I informed my family members that my friend had been missing since last night. In the noon prayer, the boy's dad shared the issue with everyone in the masjid.

The worst thing was that after hearing such a bad news everyone only horizontally nodded their heads due to despair. The Imam of the masjid promised to arrange a "Special Prayer" so that God would help my friend's dad find his son. However, I was not happy with the Imam's decision because he should have requested the villagers to expedite pragmatic action to help find my friend – rather than putting the responsibility on God. The prayers of the villagers would have

THE EXPLOITATION OF SOCIAL STATUS

been more effective if they had actually searched for my friend.

I was thinking as though God would send down angels for help. I had such thoughts because Allah helps those who take real action first rather than merely praying and waiting for others to act or for a divine miracle to happen. Nevertheless, the Imam had to continue his usual religious practices while ignoring to ask the villagers to use their God-gifted abilities and find the missing boy.

Although the villagers expressed their sympathy to my friend's dad, as I still remember his words, he later said, "I do not need this sympathy, what I need is only a real helping hand to help me find my son. I need truth, and I need harmony from the villagers to quickly resolve the case of the stolen fan by finding out the real culprit, I am fed up."

To everyone's surprise, the thief revealed himself the next day by returning the fan to the Imam of the masjid and requesting that his identity be kept hidden from the villagers. Nonetheless, it was eventually discovered that two teens had stolen the fan rather than one. Interestingly, one was the son of the Village Head "Malak," and the other was the son of the man who had raised the matter, a disciplined performer of five times prayers and caretaker of the masjid.

Even after discovering the names of the actual thieves, no one in the community reacted or claimed a thing. This is because both criminals were the sons of prominent and socially influential people in the village. At this point, my friend's dad exposed that even the Mullah himself was in a hurry to put a full stop to the issue as soon as possible – since he could not leverage the matter anymore, given that the fan was stolen by the sons of the village's elites.

On the other hand, my friend and his poor family suffered the repercussions of this saga caused by the village's hierarchal leadership structure, which was controlled and led by the village elites. However, some educated villagers discussed and condemned several times the silence of the rest of the villagers over the theft by the sons of the Malak and the other faithful person and asked for compensation. However, the elders used to claim that it was impolite and against the societal norms to question the Malak and that faithful person or speak against them for what their sons had done.

Unfortunately, nobody ever spoke about the consequences my innocent friend and his poor family – especially his dad had to bear. While they never thought or cared about the suffering of my friend and his family, who suffered harshly the brunt of this traumatic false story – created against my friend by the faithful person and due to the exploitation of the authority of the village's Malak. Despite all this drama, Malak and the other faithful person blatantly supported their sons, for they were young and had to be forgiven.

Two days after the identification of the thieves, we finally found my friend. He was hiding in his aunt's house. After meeting him, we were desperate to listen to his story and were curious to know how he managed to spend two days away from home. Because staying away from our mother at that frail age seemed so difficult for us as we all were quite young. After performing the evening prayer, as usual, we took him to the fields where we all (friends) gathered for a short while after every evening prayer.

When we asked him what had happened, he said, "I left home because I was too depressed by the villagers' taunting stigma that called me a masjid thief. I never wanted to get beaten up by the villagers for being a thief of the masjid while no one believed the truth I speak."

He added, "I also feared the punishment of a mob of villagers." Since the villagers considered him a thief and someone who had stolen from a sacred place like masjid – which was, according to the mainstream beliefs, considered an unforgivable sin. "This was the main reason I even attempted suicide when I went to the terrace of my aunt's house that evening," – said my friend. Nevertheless, hearing about his decision to commit suicide at such a fragile age drove all of us startled because it was pretty shocking and scary for us.

Shocked by his story, we all murmured to each other as we could not believe he would take such an action. One of our friends patted him for his bravery which sounded a little impolite. Therefore, my other friends and I yelled at him for being impolite. He thought it was fair to say something like this because he intended to mentally support our friend.

My friend said his aunt's house was a two-story building with a fabulous dusky view of the western side, especially during the sunset. While he told us his story, I drowned in thoughts of the view. I thought my friend might have gone there just because of the intention to be mentally peaceful and spend some time alone with serene nature.

After he told us what he went through, I suddenly told my other friends not to leave him alone for some time, especially when he was outside. This was also the reason all of us (friends) always had a good relationship with him when he was outside just to protect him from the harm of the villagers as well as to keep him mentally engaged - specifically to have him avoid negative and stressful thoughts.

I still remember his last words when he said, "I sometimes lie to my parents and family members because no one believes my words despite being authentic – even if I swear by the name of Allah or the Holy Quran. They all think that I am a liar. But sometimes I tell a lie because I fear my parents and other family elder members whom I think would beat me for doing or saying something without their permission or anything they do not like."

For example, hanging out with my friends or going outside without their permission. My willingness to lie is only inclined by the negative, harsh, and furious behavior of my parents and elders and the fact that none of them believe me – which makes me feel embarrassed and have a feeling of inferiority complex about myself. As a result of my low image in my family, I have a bad image in society too. No one in society believes me – they also think I am a liar and a thief – which eventually hurts my feelings and destroys my self-esteem. That is the reason I was overthinking and was mentally forced to put an end to my life at my aunt's house. Had my family supported me, I would also have a good image in the society."

This is not only my friend's experience; every other youngster from a middle-class household has a similar one. Almost every teenager from a middle-class family suffers from an inferiority complex, owing to society laws and codes that exclusively benefit the elites and religious masters. If not questioned or defied, this phenomenon will last longer.

The Bottom Line:

- As teenagers today, we live in a world where our voices are muted and asking questions is deemed a crime or a sin. The reason for this is the preservation of the social status quo. As a result, we are compelled to respect people depending on how they treat others in society.
- In the modern world, children deserve emotional support from their families, particularly their parents. Unfortunately, emotional support is always provided by unknowns, whereas knowns only provide emotional suffering.
- While accepting society's beliefs without question is socially considered a sign of respect. This, however, is apathy and torture of inner peace. And complacency is the most significant impediment to our ability to think critically.
- Elders should avoid yelling at their children for mistakes and instead encourage them to learn from those mistakes. Because if children are scolded for their mistakes, they will try to hide or lie about them the next time instead of attempting to avoid or correct them.
- Our society misunderstands the terms introvert, alone, and antisocial. These are considered negative characteristics by society. However, people become introverted because their words are not heard and not understood, and their feelings are not respected and valued. People isolate themselves from the crowd because they have lost faith in others, and their trust has been broken. Therefore, they find peace in solitude. Eventually, people become antisocial due to becoming victims of cultural beliefs and standards. This type of people, however, is not antisocial; instead, they are anti-societal drama and fraudulent faces.

Bibliography

Abbasi, D. R. (2009). *Women and Education in Islam*. Retrieved from Minhaj.org: https://www.minhaj.org/english//tid/8535/Women-Education-in-Islam-article-by-dr-raheeq-ahmad-rahiq-ahmed-abbasi-nazim-e-aala-mqi-minhaj-ul-quran.html

Alam, M. (2022). *The Quran Nurtures Intellect and Shapes Reason*. Retrieved from Islami City: https://www.islamicity.org/21598/the-quran-nurtures-intellect-and-shapes-reason//

Flaubert, G. (2023). *Brainy Quote*. Retrieved from https://www.brainyquote.com/authors/gustave-flaubert-quotes

Kohli, S. (2020). *Are women stronger than men? Here are 8 scientific facts to put this debate to rest*. Retrieved from Health Shots: https://www.healthshots.com/mind/are-women-stronger-than-men-here-are-8-scientific-facts-to-put-this-debate-to-rest/

Maro. (2007). *Is there any 'blind Faith" in islam?* Retrieved from Religiousforums.com: https://www.religiousforums.com/threads/is-there-any-blind-faith-in-islam.46039/

Mindfullness.org. (1997). *The Fourteen Mindfulness Trainings*. California: The Mindfulness Bell.

Tucson, M. (2023). *Dress Code for Women based on Quran*. Retrieved from Masjidtucson.org: https://www.masjidtucson.org/submission/perspectives/women/dresscode.html

Sadaqat, S, A. A. (2023). Anecdotes for Reflection Part 2. 24. Contemplation. https://www.al-islam.org/anecdotes-reflection-part-2-sayyid-ali-akbar-sadaaqat/24-contemplation

CPS International Centre for Peace & Spirituality. (2023). CPSGlobal.org. https://www.cpsglobal.org/content/does-islam-teach-people-be-close-minded

www.ingramcontent.com/pod-product-compliance
Lightning Source LLC
Chambersburg PA
CBHW020423220526
45464CB00002B/542